JOURNEY TOWARDS THE *light*

SUZANNE HASLAM

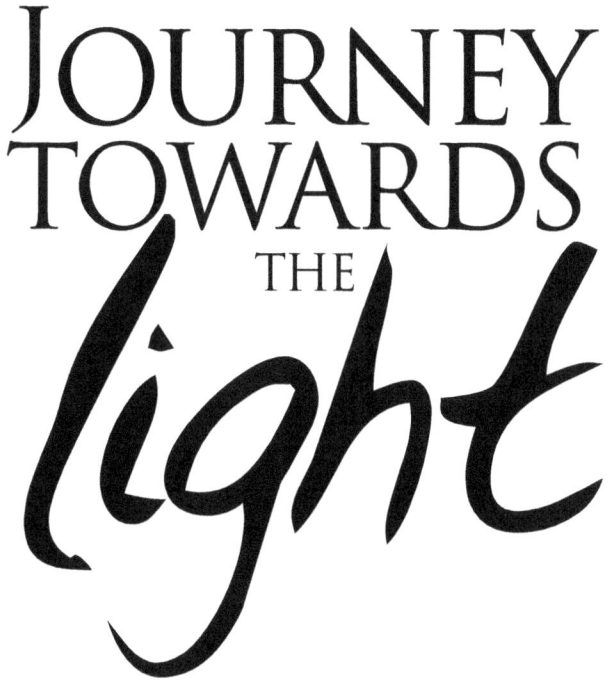

SUZANNE HASLAM

EDITED BY CHRIS NEWTON

MEMOIRS
Cirencester

Published by Memoirs

MEMOIRS

Memoirs Books
25 Market Place, Cirencester, Gloucestershire, GL7 2NX
info@memoirsbooks.co.uk www.memoirsbooks.co.uk

Copyright ©Suzanne Haslam, June 2011

First published in England, June 2011

ISBN 978-1-908223-08-1

All rights reserved.

No part of this publication may be reproduced, stored in a retrieval system, or transmitted in any form or by any means, electronic, mechanical, photocopying, recording or otherwise without the prior permission of Memoirs.

Printed in England

Contents

CHAPTER 1	The end of a marriage	Page 1
CHAPTER 2	Leaving	Page 15
CHAPTER 3	Spiritual Awakenings	Page 20
CHAPTER 4	Aftermath	Page 29
CHAPTER 5	Majorcan sanctuary	Page 37
CHAPTER 6	The Puig	Page 41
CHAPTER 7	A helping hand from Spirit	Page 55
CHAPTER 8	Making contact	Page 64
CHAPTER 9	Positive and negative	Page 72
CHAPTER 10	Escaping from the past	Page 82
CHAPTER 11	A fresh start	Page 89
CHAPTER 12	The journey home	Page 99

ABOUT SUZANNE HASLAM

Suzanne Haslam lives in Cheshire with her partner George and young son Jacob, Billy the dog and Annie the cat. Apart from working as a part-time midwife and inspirational speaker on issues surrounding domestic violence, most of Suzanne's time is devoted to caring for Jacob, who was diagnosed with cerebral palsy in May 2011. She is currently writing a further book inspired by Spirit and her son for parents whose children have additional needs, which will deal with how, as parents and citizens, we can help them to reach their full potential.

If you would like to share your experiences with Suzanne please email her at suzanne@author-suzannehaslam.co.uk
or see her website www.author-suzannehaslam.co.uk

ACKNOWLEDGMENTS

I would like to give a special 'thank you' to the following for inspiring or supporting me:

George, Ursula Harding and Lilian, Debbie and Emma Hartell, Jane Francis and family, my late grandmother Molly Bramhall, Sally Parkinson and family, Beatrice Talma, Helene and Lynda, Derek and Gwen Acorah, Sally Sharpley, Lorraine Perry & family.

I would also like to thank Chris Newton and Tony Tingle at Memoirs Books for all their time and effort in helping in the production of the book. I couldn't have done it without you.

DEDICATION

This book is dedicated to all the healers and helpers of the spirit world. In the bleakest of times you were always there for me – a massive thank you.

I would like to make a special dedication to my late grandmother Marion Emery, who has always been there for me and who unfailingly continues to support me – you are simply my special 'guardian angel' – thank you.

Chapter 1

The end of a marriage

As I sat in the waiting room listening for the call to see my GP, I was trying desperately to stay calm and controlled. It was no use. My body was shaking uncontrollably and sweat was pouring off me.

"The doctor will see you now, Suzanne," said the receptionist, and I made my way unsteadily into the room. I had brought my friend Andrea from work with me, but now I asked her to stay in the waiting room so that I could talk to the doctor in confidence. He had always been a wonderful doctor to me and my family, the old-fashioned type who always had the time for us and knew each of us personally. But as I sat on the chair, I could barely get the words out.

"I'm leaving my husband," I mumbled.

I could tell that he was horrified at the state I was in. I was seriously ill, emotionally and mentally.

"You need some time off" he said. "I'll give you a sick note."

"Thank you" I replied. That was all. I got to my feet and walked out.

I can tell you the exact date and time when my life changed forever; 5 pm on March 19, 1998. That was the moment when I took the first step towards leaving the husband who had been abusing me for the past nine years. They call it domestic abuse these days, the one-in-four statistic. I had become that one in four, that cold statistic. I had been on an emotional and mental meltdown for quite some time, but just hadn't realised it.

As I walked home, thoughts were flooding into my head. How was I going to do this? Where would I go? Where would I stay? How would I live? One thing was certain - I knew I would have do it very carefully to prevent any more damage to myself and my health. I would have to do it as safely and quietly as possible.

Chapter 1

Oddly enough, some six hours previously I had felt fine. I had known that morning that I had to leave him, could sense that if I didn't it would get physical. I had arranged to meet Andrea at her home that afternoon. I trusted her and knew she would be able to advise me.

She asked me whether I was frightened of him, and I told her I was terrified. "Leave him," she said. "You have to go."

That was all I needed – a few words of strength, a glimmer of hope and support, to tell me I was doing the right thing, to enable me to leave the situation behind forever.

I had rung my mother straight after the appointment, telling her of my decision and explaining that the relationship had not been what she might have imagined. On the way back I stopped at my parent's house, went in and sat on the sofa. I was feeling a rising sense of panic. I was terrified. My pulse was running at 160 and I was sweating profusely. I began to feel the onset of the first of many panic attacks. I couldn't breathe. I just kept saying over and over "I don't feel well, please help me".

My mum didn't really know what to say or do; she just said "Oh well, if you're happier without him".

Looking back, the onset of my breakdown was like a lid being taken off a giant pressure cooker. It had been simmering and bubbling away for some time. Telling those close to me about the abuse had somehow allowed it to lift right off. Now it was all in the open, and I was no longer hiding from the truth about my marriage. My mind and my body had had as much as they could take. I had to get out – just to survive.

The night before seeing the doctor I had told John that I was going to take a break from the relationship for a few days. In reality I was slowly edging out of it altogether. He seemed taken aback and a bit confused, as if like he didn't know what was happening. I had then left to spend the evening with a friend. So it was with a sense of dread that I walked back home that day after seeing the doctor.

John was waiting for me. He said nothing, but his body language spoke

Chapter 1

volumes. The silence felt even worse than the barrage of abuse I'd been getting. At least with verbal abuse it's out in the open - you know where you stand, what they are thinking, how bad it's going to be.

I crept into the spare bedroom and put myself to bed. I don't think I had more than an hour's sleep that night. Most of the time I just lay there, praying he would leave me alone. I stayed still and quiet as I had done so many times before - a survival technique, you might call it.

I didn't leave straight away; I needed to do it slowly. I suppose I was managing the situation, managing him, managing myself. I was also trying to hang on to what was left of my health. I later learned that for survivors of domestic abuse the point of exit is the most dangerous time. That's the moment when the abuser's controlling behaviour can suddenly go over the top. At all costs I had to avoid a sudden crisis.

How far would he go? What further damage could he do to me? I felt absolutely terrified.

We had got married on October 21, 1988, with all the hopes and dreams of every married couple. We'd been happy, at first. We had been together a good two years before we tied the knot, and he had been respectful and courteous. I had no reason to worry about having a relationship with him, no seeds of doubt, no misgivings.

Over the next five years, that all changed.

We married fairly young – I was 20, he was 24 - but it felt right. We got hitched at the local registry office with just a handful of guests - money was scarce and I didn't want anything elaborate anyway. I've never liked a big fuss. I had just entered my second year as a student nurse, and he was out of work. But we were happy, and he treated me well.

We weren't in a position to buy our own place, so we moved into a flat above my parents' shop and he started working for them. They had built up a thriving retail business through sheer hard graft, and looking back I suppose they felt obliged to give him work to help both of us out. He was to carry on working for them for the next 16 years.

We bought our first home a couple of years later, a little two-bedroomed

Chapter 1

house on a new estate. My parents were so impressed by it that they bought their own home there a year later, so by the time we split they were living round the corner from us.

John got on well with my folks - he liked them and they liked him. His family lived abroad, and I think my parents made more of an effort because he didn't have the support of his own family around him. They took him under their wing, in effect.

His parents were decent hardworking people with a lot of time for me, and for us as a couple. We would try and visit them in his home country at least twice a year and his mum would always make a big fuss of us and go out of her way to make me feel part of the family. He had a sister, who was married and was also living abroad. I met her only twice. She was a decent, quiet, unassuming person, and we got on well together.

His dad, however, had quite a temper, and I would sometimes witness violent rows between his parents, both at their home and in the shop they ran. It must have been normal for them. His mum always looked sullen and unhappy, as if she was putting up with a great deal from him. I was there once when his father called her a 'fucking shit' to her face. I just kept my head down and made myself scarce. I never saw John defend his mother.

His sister came to visit us once, not long after we got married. I had noticed that she was taking an extraordinary amount of medication, so much that she needed a seven-day pill reminder case. She must have been on around 10 pills a day. I never knew what they were for. She didn't have any medical disability or condition as far as I could see, although I did overhear something about a depression and anxiety-related illness. It wasn't my business to ask, so I didn't. I was just concerned with making her stay comfortable and enjoyable.

We had been married two years when I began to notice a change in John's behaviour towards me. He started doing and saying things that made me feel uncomfortable. He began to complain about the number of

Chapter 1

times we were having sex, and even write it down. There was nothing jokey about the way it was put over. Something had to be badly wrong.

One day I managed to summon up the courage to ask my mum about it. "Don't worry about it," she said. "Most men complain." I just took her advice, thinking that she probably knew best, being mum and all. I know now that it wasn't normal, but at the time I felt that she was older and more experienced, so she must have been right.

It wasn't Mum's fault; her answer had been based on her own limited experience. But it got worse. John became more and more demanding, until sex became an act of self-gratification, for him only; loveless, and at times forced, particularly towards the end of the relationship.

He had also started to become extremely forceful and domineering towards me. If there were decisions to be made, he would lay down the law to me. Usually he had the final say. I wasn't allowed a voice - there was no listening, no compromise.

I would have liked us to make decisions together, as a couple, but that wasn't his way at all. "We're not going out with Mike and Jane next week" he'd say, or "I don't like that sofa, it's got to go." Or he would try to stop me going somewhere – I liked going to the local garden centre (I love flowers), but he didn't like me going on my own. "Why don't you just listen to what I've got to say and do it my way!" he would shout at me, on and on. In the end I would just sit there in silence, feeling prepared to do anything for a quiet life.

He'd flip from one extreme to another, almost a Jekyll and Hyde. One week he'd have a go at me, the next he'd bring me flowers and say he was sorry for what he'd put me through. I found this really confusing, not knowing what was coming next. Looking back, I think it was this that did the most damage to my health. He was doing my head in. I couldn't cope with it; there was no stability, no predictability. I just didn't know where I was, who I was, any more.

Chapter 1

Eventually I suggested that perhaps we should seek counselling with Relate. I suppose I was trying to somehow sort things out and make things better between us, trying all avenues so to speak. Surprisingly, enough he agreed. He even seemed quite keen.

On the day of our appointment with the Relate counsellor, John had been relatively calm and normal and had stayed quiet in the car on the way there. The woman showed us into a room and explained the proceedings. We sat down and immediately the quietness vanished, and there came a torrent of verbal abuse. I was the root cause of our problems, he said. The counsellor tried valiantly to mediate the conversation, but there was only one person who was going to speak in that room, and that was John. I just sat there in shock, listening to the assault.

"If she just did as she was told there would be no problem!" he shouted. "She just needs to shut up and listen to what I've got to say!"

The truth was I hadn't said a word all day - for months, in fact. I felt prepared to do anything for a quiet life. The counsellor didn't seem unduly perturbed by his outbursts, but perhaps she was used to it and could accept it. If it happened today I think alarm bells would have been ringing – she would have recognised the signs of a controlling, abusive relationship.

After that I knew there was no hope between us. He was beyond any reasonable hope of compromise or normal behaviour.

Nobody sets out to be abused or hurt. It all happened so insidiously, a progressive build-up over time of small incidents that slowly but surely increased in frequency, momentum and intensity. By the end I had no self-esteem or confidence whatsoever. The almost continual barrage of abuse had taken away my personality, my identity as a human being.

The abuse went on like this for seven years. It wasn't until the final 12 months that I really began to appreciate that it couldn't go on. I could no longer cope with his behaviour. Deprived of love and care, I began to dislike him as a person.

Chapter 1

Something else happened that made me appreciate what I had been missing. I became friendly with a colleague I had met at the hospital social club about three months before I finally decided to leave. He was a laid-back type, friendly, polite and respectful towards me – qualities I hadn't seen for a long time. One night we became intimate. It didn't go too far – just a kiss - and we both went home alone, but a light had switched on inside me. He had given me a glimpse of how a relationship could be. That encounter didn't come to anything, but it did inspire me to make the preparations for leaving, at last, the dead relationship I was trapped in.

John was becoming visibly angrier and angrier. He was constantly starting arguments, then going out of control.

Then something else happened which helped me to make my mind up. I had a dog called Benson, whom I'd bought as a little puppy from the RSPCA. He had been one of six found in an old sack on the outskirts of my home town. He was the runt of the litter, and knew I had to have him. Benson and I had become inseparable, he desperate for a secure home while I was desperate for something, anything, to love and care for. We made a great team. Of course that didn't go down at all well with John, who quickly became intensely jealous of our relationship. It was mutual – Benson didn't like him either.

One evening a few weeks after Benson arrived, I woke from my sleep – I had been on nights - and started to go downstairs when I heard John's voice from the kitchen. He was speaking with such malevolence and hatred that I stopped in my tracks. As I stood straining to hear what he was saying, I realised he was talking to Benson. I tiptoed downstairs and looked into the kitchen to see my puppy cowering in terror in the corner, John standing over him.

"You fucking stupid bastard dog" he hissed. "I'll fucking sort you out." It was horrible to hear. The words were shocking, the voice pure evil.

I kept still for a moment, tried to steady my nerves. Then I did my best

Chapter 1

to walk into the kitchen as if nothing had happened.

"Is everything all right?" I asked.

"Yes, all fine," said John. "What would you like for tea, love?"

It was hard to believe that he could talk like that after what I had just seen and heard. He was so cunning. If I hadn't had seen it for myself, I wouldn't have had a clue what he had just done.

I called Benson to me and took him into the lounge to reassure him. After that I made sure he was with me all the time.

I felt John could have done what he liked to me - beat me, even murdered me - but I knew I would never, ever let him hurt my dog. It may seem strange to give an animal more value than you do to yourself, but as any animal lover will tell you'll do anything to protect them when it comes to danger.

Fortunately for both Benson and me we had now been given a glimpse of what he was capable of. We had seen the hidden personality within. I knew then that I had to get out, for both our sakes.

Around this time I began to become aware of something or someone with me; a presence, so to speak. I didn't know what it was – I just felt a presence watching over me, urging me to witness his behaviour. My senses seemed to have become heightened for no reason. Right up to the day I finally left, I felt someone or something was there by my side.

Even odder, ornaments started moving around, or disappearing altogether only to turn up back in their usual places. At first it was simply annoying. It carried on even when John was away on business and I was the only person who had access to the house.

There was one incident which really spooked me. As I lay on my bed upstairs, I heard what sounded like the rustling of pages, as if someone was reading a newspaper down in the kitchen. Eventually I managed to gather enough courage to edge downstairs to inspect the lounge and kitchen. Of course, there was no-one there. No window was open, and

Chapter 1

there was no sign of a forced entry. It really unnerved me. I still have no explanation for it.

The realisation that I was going to somehow have to leave him plunged me into a terrible state. The night after I saw my GP, I started having nightmares. I'd drop off to sleep only to wake up in sheer terror, building up to a panic attack. I felt seriously ill, but couldn't understand why. When I checked my pulse it was right up to 180, twice what it should have been. I felt the whole of my body was on overdrive, that I was pumped full of adrenalin, and I couldn't control it.

Just 24 hours beforehand I had felt quite normal, with no indication of stress. I had been holding down a good job, running a household, doing all the normal things normal people do. I had felt physically fit, thanks to walking 15 miles a week with Benson. That had all gone. My health had undergone a dramatic change for the worse.

I began to feel an immense, dark stress in my head. I felt I had to readjust myself physically and mentally to survive from minute to minute. My brain felt raw and vulnerable. I found myself struggling to control the most basic functions. Everything I did became a mammoth task, even brushing my teeth or washing my hair. It seemed ridiculous to be challenged by such simple things.

I remember how I coaxed myself through the simple steps of shampooing and rinsing my hair. "All you need to do is put the shampoo on your hand and then on your head and then rinse it off" I told myself. I had to do it all in slow motion, with me mentally choreographing every step. Ridiculous! What would normally have taken five minutes took the best part of an hour. I felt terrified. I hadn't got a clue what was happening to me.

I found that the more I tried to do, the more the stress in my head intensified. It was as if someone was constantly putting on the brakes, telling me "Stop! You can go no further!" It was as if I was having to do a risk analysis for every little step I needed to take. Even making a cup of tea seemed almost impossible, not least because my hands were shaking so much.

Chapter 1

Not long after I saw the doctor, a colleague at work gave me the phone number of a local medium. She was Lilian Harrison, a local woman who had been born with a gift for mediumship and was well known in the area for her talent. She would never charge for her services - if you did offer money, it went straight to charity.

Someone must have been watching over me when I phoned to make an appointment. Normally you had to join a 12-month waiting list, but there had been a cancellation, so I was lucky enough to be able to see her later that week.

I found the house and knocked nervously on the door. It opened to reveal a small lady in her seventies, with grey curly hair. She invited me in. The house had a warm and cosy atmosphere.

I was shocked at what she told me. She said that I was in a really bad marriage and that I would soon be leaving my husband. She said that my grandma was very close to me and would be helping me, and that her spirit had been trying to communicate that support around the home – for example, by making ornaments go missing. She explained to me that she had been through the same sort of experience, but in her case she had to wait until her husband had died to be free of him, as in her day divorce was unthinkable. I felt sad for her. She was such a nice lady.

I was even more shocked when she said meekly: 'They say you have been a bit naughty." She said she knew that a couple of months before I had met a man at a club. I felt myself squirming in embarrassment. How on earth could she have known that? No one knew about it apart from me and the man I had met, and she didn't know me from Adam. She told me that it was OK and pointed out that he had boosted my confidence, which was exactly what I felt.

That evening with Lilian was pivotal for me. I was shocked at how much she knew that she couldn't possibly have found out the normal way. I had long felt there must be something more "out there", as I had been

Chapter 1

attending my own local spiritualist church in Macclesfield since I was 17. I had always wondered how the mediums on the platform could communicate with those who had passed over, and would sit their mesmerised. I don't remember how and when I entered the church the first time - it just seemed to me a normal thing to do at the time.

Lilian was truly a lovely lady. Little did I know that she would eventually become a good friend, as well as a mentor to me on spiritual matters.

She told me that for a while things would be very black for me, but that I had to keep going. We made an appointment for six months later, and I thanked her and left.

I started to prepare for my exit. First I had to find somewhere to stay. I asked at the hospital about a room, but of course they didn't allow dogs and there was no way I was going to leave Benson. I couldn't afford to rent.

Somehow I had to discuss with John the arrangements for the split. It would have been much easier if he had been willing to move out and leave me in the house, but I knew that wouldn't happen. He started pricing up every little item in the home, right down to the smallest piece of bric-à-brac, and spent hours jotting everything down on paper as if he was planning some sort of military operation.

He had become increasingly fanatical about material matters, particularly over the previous 12 months. Naturally he held the purse strings. He always wanted to know what money I was spending and where it went. During cold spells in winter I would sit freezing to death, because to him, heat was a waste of money. We weren't exactly short - we both had reasonably well-paid jobs. It was just another way for him to exercise control.

In the end we agreed to sell the house. I didn't show the estate agent round - I couldn't deal with the stress.

I had managed to ring work to tell them that John and I were separating

Chapter 1

and I would need a couple of weeks off. My colleagues were shocked. He had always appeared the model husband in front of them. "Are you sure it's what you want?" they would say. "Can't you work it out somehow?" They had no idea what sort of a person John really was, and how he had been treating me.

I began to edge out of the home, one night at a time, staying at Mum's. I was trying to let him down slowly, partly to minimise the anger and the risk of aggression.

John had a black briefcase which he always took to work with him, and something about it had made me suspicious. Why would he need a briefcase for the job he did? And why did he cling on to it as if it had the Crown Jewels inside? It was always by his side, always firmly closed.

Until the morning I moved out. That's when he slipped up. He popped out to the shops, leaving it unattended.

I had to find out what was inside it. I fumbled with the locks and it popped open. My heart was racing. What if he came back and found me? I kept peering out of the window to see if he was coming down the road.

Inside was a great pile of leaflets. They were all about the same thing - how to control and manipulate others to get what you want from life - how to con people. They seemed to have come from America. He had obviously ordered them by mail.

What had he been up to? What had he been doing to me - and others?

I told my mum and dad what I had found. I felt they had a right to know who they were dealing with, especially as he was still working for them in the family business. They said nothing, but I wondered what they might now be thinking about our separation and my soon-to-be ex-husband.

Although I felt exhausted, I was only managing to sleep for about an hour a night. My brain was like an overloaded computer, working desperately to try to process what had been pumped into it and find the

Chapter 1

answers to all the questions in my head. It was as if I was trying to repair and retrain my brain. I was trying desperately to make sense of it all, find out why I felt the way I did.

It would be two more long years before I would be able to get even two hours' sleep a night. Sleeping pills didn't work - they just made me dizzy, made me feel I couldn't cope. I suppose I was living on pure adrenalin. I knew that in time I would begin to calm down, that the flow of adrenalin would slow and I would get some sleep, but that time seemed a long way off.

I was smoking 80 cigarettes a day, which in hindsight, couldn't have helped my condition. At least the smoking gave me a yardstick to my recovery in the years that followed, as I watched the figure dropping.

Those early days were unrelentingly black, bleak and frightening. Fortunately, there always seemed to be a short period each day when I felt better, and the dark stress across my head would lift. At first it would only last 15-30 minutes, but as the months went by it gradually increased. By the time a year had gone by I could expect to feel OK for as much as an hour, even two. At these times I would go for a walk or a short swim, which all seemed to help. But always the stress would return, reminding me to tread carefully, to limit my stress levels.

I felt acutely aware of everything around me, of every little detail of my feelings and my physical and mental responses. This made the experience even more frightening. The mere mention of the phrase "nervous breakdown" would conjure up images of white-gowned patients doing time in some institution, completely out of it and heavily medicated. During my nursing training I often had encounters with patients who could have been a danger to themselves and others because of their mental state. The most disturbing case I saw was a young mum sectioned to the local psychiatric hospital because she had lost her baby to cot death. She had completely lost control. She was totally unaware of anything around here

Chapter 1

and seemed to be constantly fighting off imaginary ants. After about six months in hospital she did eventually recover, but having seen what a breakdown could do to you I was terrified that I might go the same way.

I was very tearful about how bad I felt physically and mentally and felt constantly drained by it all. I felt all the time that I was trying to keep my head above water, trying to hold on to my sanity. The worst part was knowing that this illness wasn't going to disappear overnight. I knew it would be a long time before I would be able to get myself back on an even keel and lead some sort of normal life.

Chapter 2

Leaving

Within a week of the initial split, I had moved into my parent's home, just me and a bag of essentials. I was grateful for a roof over my head, but it did nothing to ease the stress. My sister Sara was also living there temporarily, following a house move. She was busy looking for somewhere to live, but all I could do was keep my head down. It had to be one move at a time.

I never really told Mum and Dad what John had done, at least not to begin with. Talking about it, defending my actions and how he had behaved, would only have pumped the stress levels up again.

My dad was oblivious to it all. I think he quite liked the idea of the family being back together again under one roof. Because I was a nurse, he took the opportunity to talk constantly about the various ailments he had, completely unaware of how I was feeling. In the end I just had to say I couldn't deal with it anymore - I felt too ill myself. This only compounded the stress, because I felt guilty about not being more helpful.

It was a busy household, with the rest of the family constantly coming and going, but at least I had a room to retreat to. I didn't have to think about putting food on the table; I did try to cook something one night for all of us, but it ended up in the bin. I just couldn't do it. Just a simple cooked meal, but it was almost as if I had forgotten how to do it, hadn't the confidence to make it work. I felt so frustrated, as I had always taken pride in my cooking.

He would turn up every day at my Mum's with his usual charm, pretending to be the model husband, despite all that had happened. "When are you coming back?" he would ask me. Unbelievable - I think he really imagined I would go back. I knew better than to contradict him

Chapter 2

outright. I would just say that I would be staying a bit longer at Mum's, knowing full well I'd never be going back. I was trying to do it all as slowly and gently as I could.

At least one thing went right. Within two weeks of our putting the house on the market, it was sold. Mum and I went over to blitz the whole house clean for the people moving in. I couldn't do too much as I felt so ill and exhausted. I saw the sale of the house as an end to a chapter in my life and a farewell to the dreadful atmosphere that had accumulated within its walls, one I never wanted to live through again.

Mum and Dad, my sister and the rest of the family were all still treating John as if nothing had happened. I had explained to them that he hadn't exactly been a model husband and my mum, at least, could see how ill I was. But as soon as they weren't around his behaviour reverted back to what it had been, and all the hate and malice reappeared.

Just before our buyers moved in that summer, I went back to the house to cut the grass and tidy the garden up, as it was beginning to look a little overgrown. Mum decided she would work at the front while I tackled the lawn at the back.

I had no sooner started cutting the grass when John appeared at the back door. Suddenly he took off and ran towards me with a look of pure hatred on his face. I cowered in terror. I really thought he was going to take a swing at me.

He stopped right in front of me, thrusting his face into mine, intimidating me as he knew how to do so well.

"Everything ok?" he said sarcastically. There was a horrible smirk on his face. He knew exactly what he was doing - pressing all my buttons, proving that he could still control me, determined to scare the living daylights out of me.

I was terrified and shouted for Mum, who appeared from the front garden. In an instant he was the charming son-in-law again.

Chapter 2

"Everything's fine, Tina" he told her. "You're doing such a great job with the garden." She's missed it again, I thought. He's too clever for her.

But not everyone was so easily fooled. One day just before I left for good, Andrea dropped in. John was there too, making lunch, and of course when Andrea arrived he was the model husband all over – attentive, charming, even offering her some lunch.

Fortunately for me Andrea had been there before. She saw right through him.

"I know what he's up to," she said. "He's very clever." She had gone through a similar experience in a relationship about three years earlier, and knew how to see behind the niceness. That made me feel much better. I was extremely relieved.

Sometimes while I was staying with them, Mum would take me out. We liked to visit the local garden centres, buying plants and having a bite to eat. I was happy to tag along with her, glad to be getting beyond the four walls of the house to try and take my mind off how bad I was feeling. Yet at first I found these outings very stressful. Venturing out of the house was a terrifying trip into the unknown, and usually no sooner had we arrived at our destination than I started wanting to go back home.

I don't think Mum really understood - how could she? She wasn't feeling what I was feeling, didn't know what I'd been through. All I knew was that I couldn't take the hustle and bustle of the cars and people around me. The stress and the pressure were building up inside my head until I had no choice but to insist on baling out and heading for home. I was overloading my brain when it needed as much rest as possible.

Now I had to think about divorce. Escaping from the house was only the first step. I knew I had to free myself from John and all the connections I had with him, and that only by divorcing him, by getting him totally out of my life, would I be able to recover fully.

It took me eight attempts to pluck up the courage to ring a solicitor and start divorce proceedings. Not that I wasn't sure I wanted a divorce – I

Chapter 2

just had to overcome the terrible stress I was feeling.

Shelley, the solicitor, was a tall young woman who clearly didn't put up with any messing around either in her professional affairs or her personal life. She proved, in fact, to be a great role model for me.

She didn't need me to explain to her what had really gone on in the marriage. She knew. She could tell by the way I looked, by the shaking hands, by the body language. She had seen it all before.

Mum accompanied me to all the meetings with her. At first I was only able to give her snippets of what had happened to me, because it just seemed too stressful to talk about it. Eventually I was able to give her the examples she needed for the evidence, to enable her to arrange a divorce on grounds of unreasonable behaviour. She needed 10 examples of such behaviour to present to the judge. I could have given her 30.

She sorted the divorce out quickly and efficiently. I was never left alone with him in court; she was always by my side. Most important of all, she believed me.

Within two weeks of my breakdown, I was back at work. I knew I had to get back in harness. Some might think it was all too soon, but for me it was the right thing to do.

That's not to say I felt I had recovered - I felt terrible. Always there was that feeling of dark pressure in my head, of impending doom. I was feeling constant, unrelenting anxiety and my heart rate was still going up to 180 and never below 120 - I was still on overdrive.

I didn't relish the thought of going back, but I knew I had to. I knew that if I didn't do it soon I wouldn't do it at all, and that would have been the end of my nursing career and the end of my independence. It was a career I'd worked hard for and enjoyed.

Going back to work would be an important step in regaining my self-confidence and getting back into normality. On top of that it was a matter of financial survival, as I knew I would not be able to stay at my parents' home indefinitely and there would be rent or a mortgage to pay.

Chapter 2

In the days leading up to going back to work I did all I could to help myself. I bought essential oils, bache, herb and plant extracts and countless relaxation tapes - anything I could get my hands on that claimed to reduce stress levels and aid relaxation. I don't think they did much for me, certainly not at first, but at least I was doing something to help myself.

On the day of my return, my head was pounding, my pulse was racing and no doubt I was trembling. I was terrified about how my colleagues would react, what they would say and above all what they would think of the state I was in. Finally, with horrendous anxiety, pounding head and a pulse rate even higher than usual, I plucked up what was left of my courage and walked back into the hospital again.

I needn't have worried about the reaction. I will never forget all the kindness and understanding which was shown to me in those early days back at work. The support I got was amazing - and what a difference it made to the way I felt. Some of my colleagues had gone through divorce themselves, so they knew I was just going through the inevitable bad patch and the feelings it brings with it. They didn't know that I had actually gone through a breakdown.

Thankfully they steered me away from the stressful cases and just allowed me the space and time to deal with the ordinary work day by day. I was extremely fortunate.

About six weeks after my return, I tested myself on a new blood-pressure machine; the reading was 190/120. It made me wonder what it had been at the worst time. I knew it must have been life-threateningly high.

Chapter 3

Spiritual Awakenings

Although in one way I felt as if part of my brain was shutting itself down to cope with the stress, I had also begun to realise that another part had somehow 'opened'. Something very strange seemed to have started happening to me. Like a light bulb being switched on, I began to experience something I had never felt in myself before - a psychic ability.

Like many people, I had often experienced odd coincidences – you think of a particular person and the next minute they ring you, or you bump into them. Sometimes I'd get a particular feeling about a person or situation, and it would turn out to be correct. But nothing could have prepared me for what I began to experience now. It was an awareness which stretched far beyond that of any normal person. I felt I simply 'knew' everything about everybody - I was aware of the thoughts and feelings of everyone around me. Not only did I sense these things - I had begun to experience other people's feelings. I could predict what people were going to do before they did it. I knew when someone had entered a room, even though I couldn't hear or see them. I knew what friends and family would be doing for the day. I knew what people would say before they said it. It was bizarre.

I began almost unconsciously to finish off the sentences of people I was talking to, because being a kind person I thought I'd simply help them! Not surprisingly, this rather annoyed people, so I tried to stop myself. I had to learn to shut up. It was all very strange.

I never questioned my new-found ability - I just accepted it. It soon felt comfortable and natural. I felt at ease and at one with everything and everyone around me. It became slightly boring at times, especially when you knew what was going to happen or what was about to be said. But it did come in handy too, when I had to deal with my ex-partner and my boss!

Chapter 3

My nosey neighbours would have had a field day if they had shared my ability. But I firmly believe that they would never have received such a gift anyway. I believe it was given to me first because I could be trusted with such information and knowledge, and second because it would be used only for the good of others. I'm proud of the number of people I've been able to help. My career in health care provides opportunities to make a difference to the lives of the many people I come into contact with day to day. Since then I have learned to shut down a little to protect myself both mentally and physically from others around me - to limit how much I absorb from others, so to speak.

At the time of this increased awareness I also remember sensing the most extraordinary 'healing' taking place around me. I didn't know what it meant at the time. I didn't see anything or anyone; I just knew that someone or something was giving me the most powerful healing energies that I could ever have imagined. Some people would talk about Reiki or spiritual healing energy, but I had never had such a thing before.

Looking back, I instinctively knew that there was some sort of greater power working around the clock for me. I felt it healing me, comforting me, as if it was trying to balance things for me, creating a calmness and equilibrium around and within myself. It felt like a presence around me, even though I couldn't see or hear anything at the time. The feeling would become more pronounced when I began to do things for myself, to try and relax, which was difficult at that time.

Eventually this healing power helped me enormously on my journey back to full health. It may seem that sometimes we don't feel we have the strength to take any more, but the truth is we can. We can always go on to live another day despite the odds against us. I could easily have given up, stayed in bed and shut the world out, but I knew that if I didn't try and help myself to recover I would have gone downhill fast, with no life left to speak of. I would have died within myself. Sometimes I would feel I was drowning and continually having to come up for breath, every day.

Chapter 3

I was frightened and stunned, a rabbit in the headlights.

The healing feeling really came into its own when I slipped getting out of the bath one morning. I was in agony, and could barely move. I thought I would be bedbound or immobile for weeks, just as I had started back at work. And then, overnight, I was again made aware of this tremendous healing power around me. By first light my back was completely healed. I got up to find I had full mobility, no pain, not even a twinge. It was unbelievable.

I began to realise that whatever it was that was giving me the healing had the ability to cure almost anything. At the time I remember thinking that the ability of all of us to heal really did exist. This idea was later confirmed to me by a book called Celestine Prophecy, by James Redfield, which talks of the higher spiritual levels – almost heavenly - that humans can and will attain. The book says that eventually there will be no need for medicines, because as the human race progresses towards attaining that higher state of being and spirituality they will gain the ability to heal others simply through the power of touch and thought.

This marked a new beginning for me. My mind had begun to open to the possibility of other things, other forces, which accompany us through our journey of life, all working behind the scenes for the greater good of mankind and the world itself. I never felt frightened by it all, but I did feel very small in the grand scheme of things, knowing that something very big was shaping and moulding us all. Was it God? I had no idea. I didn't really know who God was, or even whether "He" existed. He was just someone whose name came up rather often, usually around Christmas time. I remember as a child seeing pictures of Jesus in white clothing in the books we had at primary school, but that was about it. As a child I used to feel sorry for him because he'd been such a nice man and he'd had to be crucified. That bit of the story always upset me.

Now I was beginning to think not only that such a being, such a power, could actually exist, but that I had access to it myself. And it didn't mean

Chapter 3

sitting in a church week after week and having it preached to me – I was seeing concrete evidence for it.

My dog Benson was also aware of my new found psychic ability. He was tremendously affected by the energies around us – it was as if we illuminated one another. I began to find I could tune into him, and him to me, without words. He knew how I felt and what I needed at any given time. It was obvious to my friends, because their pets were not at all like that.

Benson was one of the biggest factors in helping me to recover. He came to live with me at my parents' place after the sale of the house, and it was really after this that my experiences began to escalate. I still felt ill, and the only thing that mattered to me was having somewhere I could retreat to in peace to rest and recover while I was figuring out what on earth had happened to me.

I never really slept at all for the first few years, except for the odd few hours here and there. When darkness had fallen and everyone in the house had taken to their beds, I would be lying there awake, night after night. The hustle and bustle of the day reassured me by helping me to keep in touch with normal goings-on around the home, but night-time was difficult because it was all so deathly quiet. It was at these times that the enormity of it all would hit me. I would feel horribly lonely and sad.

I felt I had a jigsaw in my head, a million and one pieces which I had to put together to work out what had happened and what I could do to make sure it never happened again. My ex had completely distorted my outlook on life and my experience of normal behaviour. I felt that I had accepted his behaviour, when anyone else would have run a mile. I had so much to learn, and at night it would overwhelm me.

At these times I began to feel that somebody was kneeling next to me in my bedroom. I couldn't see anyone - I was just aware that somebody was there. Usually it happened around four in the morning. It unnerved me a bit, but I would just continue to lie their resting. At first I thought I

Chapter 3

was imagining it, but then I began to feel somebody or something touch my hand, very softly and gently. I knew this was something extraordinary, but because it was reassuring and not threatening I felt at peace and was glad to feel that somebody or something was looking after me.

I thought at the time that it might have been my grandmother, who had died some 18 years before. I knew she was looking down on me, as I was always very close to her, and of course Lilian had said she would be looking after me. After she had died, when I was about 15, strange things would happen - I would sometimes hear rapping noises at my bedroom door. It happened to my sister and mother as well.

I always gave Gran's picture pride of place on the windowsill in my bedroom. Once I moved it out of sight because my bedroom was crammed with stuff, and was promptly told via a message through a medium at the spiritualist church that Grandma didn't like it because she couldn't see what was going on!

I realise now that she was able to see me, but she had translated it in a way that would hit home and make me think. Very clever!

I also became aware that my hair was being stroked - just a slight touch, not frightening. I know now that I was in a sense being primed, introduced to what lay ahead of me in my spiritual development. It was only the beginning.

I had no idea at the time that the experiences after my divorce would eventually be seen as a catalyst to the experiences that were about to happen to me. If anyone had told me this I simply wouldn't have believed it. My illness and suffering, coupled with the minimal support I was getting, led to somebody helping me spiritually, simply because no one else was there for me.

Sometimes people wonder why such experiences don't happen to them, but I now know that if you have a good support network and there are people there for you, you may not need such experiences to recover. In my case, Spirit, as I call it just stepped in. You are never left alone to cope on your own.

Chapter 3

Others might be petrified by such goings on. My experiences didn't really frighten me - until I began to hear the bedroom door handle moving, which did freak me out! The first time I thought it was my mum, but I opened the door to find that no-one was there. After that I never looked – I hid under the duvet!

I now know that I was being tested. Like most people I had seen films about the supernatural, and they used to terrify me. If I hadn't fed myself such rubbish I probably wouldn't have been so scared.

Odd experiences like the rattling door handle became quite normal to me in the end and I started to accept them and get used to the experiences and the presence of Spirit in my life.

Living back at home wasn't as hard as I thought it would be, but when I wasn't working I did tend to rest in my bedroom and avoid seeing my family except at mealtimes or in passing on the way to work. I just wanted to keep myself to myself.

I did notice that John seemed to be appearing a lot at the house. When I arrived back from work his car would be there on the drive, and I'd wonder what the hell he was doing there. I'd feel petrified going through the front door knowing he was inside, and would wonder how I could protect myself and my family from him.

Then I'd walk in and it would be like the bloody Waltons, all laughing and smiling as if nothing had happened. I couldn't believe it. Here he was deliberately infiltrating my family, making out as if he was some sort of saint, playing the long-lost son-in-law. Yet my folks were completely oblivious to the real John. To them he was charm personified, constantly showing an interest in them all. I was so afraid of him that I never stayed to join in - I always retired to my room. Some days I would walk round and round the block until his car had gone. I felt completely pushed out.

At times my dad would ring John up and invite to come over for a 'brew'. He would even help him with his model railway track in the loft. That went on for months, and I had to stomach it. I tried to talk to my

Chapter 3

family about it, but it fell on deaf ears. In their eyes, he could do no wrong. He was so good at hiding his real persona. They never experienced the stalking he got up to when they were away on holiday and I was on my own in the house. It would mostly happen when it was dark, either late at night or in the early hours of the morning. I'd hear him shouting or throwing stones at the window and messing around outside the house. I'd go round ritually making sure that all the curtains were drawn and all the windows and doors were closed. He knew he was frightening me to death, and that even though we were separated he was still in control.

Underneath all the niceness towards my family was a bubbling, festering anger towards me, because I had dared to leave him and take back control of my life. He never let that anger show in front of anyone else. They just thought that he too was suffering the effects of separation and divorce.

And then I started looking at my bank statements. During the last years of our marriage he had taken control of all our accounts and paid all the bills. Now I noticed that substantial amounts of cash were missing from my account. He had been transferring money from my account to his every month for the past two years.

How he had persuaded the bank to do it without my signature is still a mystery to me. I let them know what I thought, and the debits stopped immediately. The next time he visited, Mum and I asked him about it – and guess what, he said he could feel one of his migraines coming on and he would have to leave. I hadn't realised migraines could come on that suddenly!

For once my mum had taken notice. Yet nothing more was ever said about it and he was still made welcome, which I found extremely difficult to deal with. I didn't tackle it at the time - I was far too ill for a confrontation - but I knew I would have to say something eventually. I felt my family could have spared me a little more support, or at least tried to protect me from him. It was extremely painful.

Chapter 3

In the September I visited Lilian again, as arranged. The prospect of the visit provided a glimmer of hope, and I was counting the days to our meeting. She explained to me that things were still very black (I think I knew that!). She knew of the spiritual experiences I had had, especially at night, and said that around Christmas I would be getting a surprise. She didn't say what it was, just that it would open my eyes.

We agreed to meet in another six months' time. She always gave me hope and I found a strength from her that I got from no-one else at that time. She seemed so wise and knowing, and gave me enormous reassurance.

Christmas 1998 approached. Mum and Dad had planned a holiday in Thailand for the festive period, and were due to arrive back in the New Year, so I would be celebrating Christmas with my sister.

I worked on Christmas Day, while my sister spent it with her boyfriend at his parents' home. We met up on Boxing Day at my parents' home and watched the usual films on the television and played some music. Then in the evening I headed upstairs for a soak in the bath, planning to get into my pyjamas and sit down to a relaxing evening. I was still taking things slowly.

From the bathroom I could hear my sister chatting on the phone. When I came downstairs I noticed that she'd had done her usual trick of carrying the handset from the hall table into the lounge and had closed the door behind her.

I had walked into the empty sitting room to leave my sister in privacy when suddenly I became aware of something in the room with me - something which seemed to be building and growing with every second that passed, something that was making my senses heighten. The presence started to grow. I went into the dining room; it was there too. I went into the hall, and there it was again. It seemed to be flowing through the whole house, some sort of force which seemed to be gathering pace and speed.

Whatever it was, it made me feel extraordinarily elated. It felt very

Chapter 3

special. I knew it was Spirit related, and that I was at first hand experiencing the power and presence of something godly. The presence gathered momentum, and I suddenly notice that some toys in the sitting room - presents which had been left unwrapped for my nephew - had started to play of their own accord.

I stared in disbelief. Benson had immediately cottoned on that something strange was in the house and shot under the dining-room table. He was shaking with fear.

I made my way to the lounge to get my sister. As I approached the door I could see the telephone cord being whipped about. The door was shut, so it certainly wasn't my sister doing it from inside the lounge.

As I opened the door to the lounge the wire was still lashing the door. My sister just freaked out. She could see that no-one was shaking the wire, and she started to scream. I tried to calm her down, without success.

Then, all of a sudden, it stopped. The wire fell slack and the toys were silent. The house was calm again.

For a moment we just sat there in the sitting room in shocked silence. "What the hell was that?" said my sister. She was trembling, but I wasn't frightened at all. I knew we had experienced the presence of Spirit. Lilian's prediction that something special would happen had come true.

Chapter 4

Aftermath

I'd been living with my parents for a year by the time the divorce was declared absolute. It felt good that legally it was all over, but I still had to cope with the after-effects of my breakdown. My mind was still constantly on the go as I went on sorting through the mess in my head. I was examining the choices I had made in life and wondering how I could have done things differently. I still wasn't sleeping. I felt I was living on adrenalin.

Each day was an uphill struggle. My confidence and self-esteem were shattered and most of the time I felt at rock bottom. I was still in the middle of a breakdown, yet I was trying desperately to rebuild myself back into the person I had been. Every day I would do a little more to climb back towards normality – just a shopping trip or a little cleaning, perhaps a short conversation.

Slowly but surely I began to gain control of the stress. The more I tackled everyday life, the more the stress dissipated. It never stopped feeling frightening, but through sheer determination I gradually climbed back towards normality. I knew I had no choice.

Long walks with Benson helped a great deal. We would often go to the woods at Alderley Edge and sit looking out over the Cheshire plain. My few short moments of peace, the exercise and the fresh air helped greatly.

Unfortunately, as I began to feel the stress lifting, I started getting violent headaches. They were like nothing I had ever known – even the strongest painkillers couldn't touch them. I was never sick, but they'd last for hours on end. All I could do was lie down in the dark until they went away. They didn't stop until about 18 months after the start of my breakdown. I never told anyone about the headaches, but I vividly remember taking myself away from family gatherings at the time to lie down.

Chapter 4

My bedroom became a shrine to the life I had to lead to stay 'safe'. I plastered the walls with statements like "You have the right to say no" and "You have the right to be treated with respect" and would look at them every day. I was drumming everything positive I could into my conscious mind in an attempt to build the confidence and the perspective of right and wrong which I had lost.

I started reading self-help books to equip myself with the skills I needed to protect myself. I wrote down the things I found stressful, and formulated strategies to overcome them. At the time a colleague at work was constantly picking on me. Eventually I managed to tackle her and put an end to the problem. That gave me more confidence in tackling such issues. It wasn't easy, because she and others I found challenging always reminded me of my husband and the way he had frightened the life out me. My instinct was always to run, to avoid conflict, but I knew I had to tackle it.

I didn't know at the time what was happening to me, but I remember being drawn to a book at the library about breakdowns and realising from the list of symptoms that I had indeed had some sort of breakdown.

In March 1999, a year after my initial breakdown, I moved into rented accommodation. I felt I needed more independence if I was to continue recovering. I think my parents felt I should have got over the split within a few months. They simply didn't appreciate that I had suffered a breakdown and there was no way I could recover so fast.

I remember my sister threatening to take me to the doctors to "sort it out". I knew through my medical training that no doctor could take away the issues I was dealing with – only time could heal. It continues to intrigue me that people seem to imagine doctors can cure anything. There are some things we have to sort out ourselves. My sister didn't understand this at the time, but I don't begrudge her attitude because you couldn't expect her to.

The continued presence of my ex was another deciding factor in my

Chapter 4

moving out. I had to seek out some sort of peace for myself, and I was certainly never going to get it with the multitude of issues that filled my folks' home at the time. Moving out became another step forward in removing myself from John altogether.

I moved into a room at a colleague's home, which gave me the deeper peace and quiet I needed. She and her husband were a lovely couple with Christian morals and values, and they became a great support to me even though they never really appreciated my situation or what I was recovering from. I don't think they ever really wanted to know. They never tried to judge me or pry into my secrets, they just allowed me to be, which was all I needed.

They would ask me how I was, which seemed a revelation, because no-one had done that before. I realised the difference a few words of support can make – they helped me to stay positive in the darkest times. I will always be grateful to my friends for taking me under their wing and providing me with a safe environment in which to recover.

That September, in my quest for further independence and solitude, I bought a small terraced house in Macclesfield. It was a big step for me, as I had never owned a home on my own before. It needed a lot of work doing to it, but I managed to find the money with the proceeds from the divorce and the house sale. By the time I had finished doing it up it looked fabulous, with mellow, soothing colours throughout. It became my haven.

I had always been such an independent person, and all I wanted was to get back that feeling of not relying on others and living a happy life on my own. But it took time to get used to living alone, and although friends and family would call occasionally, there were times when I felt acutely lonely. Days would go by with no contact from anyone. Sometimes the sense of isolation would make me feel panicky, which only compounded the feelings of anxiety I was still trying to leave behind me.

Benson of course was a great comfort. He was quite happy about the

Chapter 4

move, but I remember that if at any time I was feeling sad, so was he. I started to take short breaks with him. We spent most of our time in the Lake District, plodding miles and miles across the mountain terrain and taking in the beauty of the hills and moors.

We'd book into a cheap bed-and-breakfast and plan our journeys together. After the evening meal we would trudge back to our digs and watch television. I still wasn't sleeping well and would often wake up feeling scared and isolated. Whenever I woke, worried or fretful over my situation, I could feel that strange presence and knew that someone was there - I just couldn't see them.

That was until one particular night in the Lakes. I woke in the early hours of the morning to catch a glimpse of both my grandma and granddad at the side of the bed next to me. They were uttering words of support and encouragement. Their forms were hazy and shadowy, but I knew it was them.

I had never in my life seen any kind of ghost or apparition, but this was proof that there is something beyond death, and I realise now how lucky I was to have experienced that. Some people want so much to see loved ones who have passed over, but never do. I've still never forgotten that morning. It was especially poignant to me as I had always been so close to my grandma. I had never known my grandfather, as he had died before I was even thought of, but he looked just like the pictures I had been shown as a child.

My holidays gave me the time I needed to think things out and the space just to be, as well as the chance to vent some of the anger I felt over what had happened to me. I'd march up those hills sometimes as if I was going to war.

To relieve the boredom of my own company, I found I was talking to myself quite a lot. It worked, because I always seemed to get the answers to the questions I needed, especially when trouble cropped up with the bills or when there were work or family-related issues. I remember one

Chapter 4

day asking my mother whether she also talked to herself about problems. She said she didn't. She probably thought I was stark raving mad, but at least she didn't freak out on me.

I started making regular visits to a spiritual church in Macclesfield. They were always so friendly there, and I needed the social contact as well as the spiritual side. Every week I would get message after message through a series of mediums who took to the platform with words of encouragement and support from Spirit. It became a bit embarrassing to get so many messages, as I felt others were far more deserving than me. I would sit and wish someone else would get a message, but week after week they kept coming for me. I wasn't ungrateful, but I would have preferred not to draw attention to myself.

One night I was startled to get a message from a male medium who said my grandma was standing next to him. He said my gran was delighted that she could talk to me, and that she had known from an early age that there was something different about me. It was at this point that it all began to click, although I did feel a bit sheepish as some of the things I had talked to myself about had been of a rather personal nature!

The medium told me that within three years I would be fully developed as a medium, and that I wouldn't be joining circles to learn the trade but would learn alone with Spirit in my own circle.

I left that night wondering what on earth was happening to me. It was all a complete mystery, but at least I felt good about it. I was intrigued more than anything - I knew a lot of learning was about to come my way.

Life went on. My recovery was a slow process, and to try to speed it up I began to read more, usually books by people who had undergone traumas of their own and told how they had rebuilt their lives. Most were of a spiritual nature, and they helped me a great deal. They also helped me to understand some of the spiritual experiences I was experiencing.

One of the most important books I read was The Celestine Prophecy

Chapter 4

by James Redfield, which I mentioned earlier. It helped to shape me as a person, because it explained why people do the things they do and why they hurt one another. It taught me how to recognise the negative traits of others and stay protected from them.

It offered me an awareness I had not received from anyone before. Before my breakdown I had been very naive in thinking everyone was as courteous as me. I now know that's not the case, and that we need to protect ourselves from certain folk - wish them well, but avoid them. That awareness is a survival technique, so to speak, for avoiding unnecessary stress exposure. At some point we will of course all come up against sadness and disappointment at the behaviour of a loved one, but it's the length of time we expose ourselves to it that does the damage. It can cost us the amazing opportunities in life that await us.

As time went by I was to experience a lot of hostility from so-called friends and colleagues. A year or so after the initial bombshell I experienced a depression, without even realising it. Others had to tell me how I had been behaving, after I 'came out' of myself. I was a little surprised to be told I had seemed depressed, as I thought I'd just gone a bit quiet. But my friends noticed telltale clues, such as my coming into work with hardly a scrap of make-up on – something I would never have done before.

What really stunned me was the fact that no-one had offered me any help or support at the time - not even a "how are you?" It seemed bizarre to me, as I would certainly have done as much for them. At the time I was exasperated by it all - as if I didn't have enough to cope with without having to endure hostility from them! It was when I started to become a little more confident that they started to become distant, as if they were cutting me off. I believe they were missing the old Suzanne, the Suzanne who had always been there for them, the Suzanne they had always poured their troubles on to and who had never asked for anything in return. The

Chapter 4

Suzanne who had always been the bubbliest person around, who could make others feel brilliant about themselves. The truth was, that Suzanne had gone.

When my depression lifted, I began to change as a person. A new me began to grow. I noticed the beginnings of a new-found confidence and strength. It wasn't the books that had done that, but the fact that I had managed to drag myself up from the depths of despair and fear I had sunk into. I was becoming the person I should have been.

Yet my friends and family didn't seem to appreciate the change. They wanted the old Suzanne back, to do things for them, to keep them strong, so to speak.

I realized that for many years I had been acting as some sort of matriarch within my family. I had been the mediator who would step in when troubles broke out, as I had been at work.

I couldn't understand why, just because I had needed to take a back seat for a while to recover, I had been deprived of the support and understanding of my friends and workmates. They couldn't have cared less - at times they even made my life a misery. I was ignored, pushed out from conversations, brushed aside. It was as if I had caused them great offence by not listening to their problems.

Although I felt I was continually growing as a person, I was still greatly affected by what had happened to me. Two years after the crisis, I was still having nightmares about it. At the time I just didn't have the energy to confront people about what they were doing to me or how it made me feel. And although I was beginning to take some steps forward in my life, there were many times when I was taking huge steps back. That pattern would continue for the first five years after my breakdown.

I also found that I had begun to avoid men - not because I hated them, but because they frightened me. I felt I hadn't had too many positive experiences where they were concerned, so they became - all of them - a no-go area. In the presence of a man I would shrink into myself. Even

Chapter 4

colleagues I had worked with for years, perfectly kind, decent men, made me run. I couldn't talk to them. It was an overreaction of course, but perhaps one I had to experience before I could get back to normality. It was to fade as time went by, as I began to build confidence and get some perspective back. I knew in my head, of course, that all men weren't really like that, but I couldn't feel it, not yet.

At times I felt I had so much to deal with that it took my breath away. There were mixtures of feelings and emotions, mostly unpleasant, which I didn't understand. It wasn't until some eight years later, while I was researching a topic for my interview for a health visitor's post, that I read about PTSD - post traumatic stress disorder - and realised that its symptoms matched the feelings I had suffered.

Although most of us are aware that PTSD affects soldiers and others who have faced conflict, it can actually affect anyone, and does. Some five per cent of men and ten per cent of women will be affected by PTSD at some point in their lives. Up to 30 per cent of people exposed to a stressful event or situation of an exceptionally threatening or catastrophic nature - such as natural disaster, torture, rape or sexual abuse - will go on to develop PTSD.

I realised I had all the symptoms - the nightmares, the flashbacks, the disturbed sleep, the avoidance of reminders, emotional numbing, the constant anxiety and heightened stress responses. In time they would all fade as I got used to life after marriage and new surroundings.

I never sought help for my symptoms. I didn't know that what I had could be labelled and treated, so I just ploughed on.

I do feel that my recovery could have been a little speedier if I had sought the right support. Fortunately the world is now more aware of the problem of PTSD, and support is available. If you suffer from it, you don't have to let it stop you living the life you deserve.

Chapter 5

Majorcan sanctuary

In June 1999 I decided that after everything I had been through I deserved some sort of a break. My parents were about to jet off to Majorca with my sister and her children, and I decided to accept their invitation to tag along.

I'd always hated flying, but this time my fear and anxiety were off the scale. My palms were sweating like mad and adrenalin was pumping round my body. I know you're more likely to be killed crossing the road, but you don't think rationally when you're engulfed with fear 32,000 feet up in the air. You sit there listening to every tiny nuance of engine sound, watching the stewards for the slightest signs of stress or worry. As a result, you're exhausted long before you've touched down at your sunshine destination. And then you spend the rest of the holiday worrying about the flight home! Not much fun.

In fact the holiday turned out to be a godsend. We were a stone's throw from the beach, and the sun shone every day. There was the inevitable family stress and tension at times, mostly caused by my sister trying to cope with her young children. Most of her frustration was taken out on me because she felt resentful that I could flit off whenever I wanted, not having children in tow. I thought, I can't even come away on holiday without someone having a go.

One morning the local holiday rep came over to the apartment to ask how things were going and whether we needed anything. I was with Mum at the time. As if she knew I was in need of some peace and relaxation, the rep told us about a local monastery in the old town of Pollensa, which sounded interesting. She gave us directions, and we decided to hire a car and take a trip up there that Thursday.

The monastery was signposted from the busy main road to Palma - the

Chapter 5

sign read "Santuario del Puig de Maria". It seemed a long way up and we were glad we'd hired a car. We drove up past a scattering of houses, mostly owned by local people, with bell-ringing goats and chickens running free.

After about half a mile the road became very narrow and twisty, so we decided to park the car and walk the rest of the way. The path was extremely steep and we kept having to stop to catch our breath.

As we climbed we began to get the most incredible views of the old town of Pollensa below us, and the traffic noise had faded almost to nothing. We could just make out the tiny dots of cars buzzing along the highway to Palma. It was so quiet – all we could hear was the birds singing in the trees.

Then the road began to disappear, leaving only a cobbled footpath up to the monastery. I spotted a cave at the side of the path, its entrance marked by a red crucifix.

It took us an hour to get to the monastery. We slumped on to a stone seat outside the building to get our breath back. After a well-earned drink from the refreshment counter we walked into the building to be met by the wonderful rustic smells of days gone by. This was an old building steeped in history. Signs requested silence, but we didn't need them - the place commanded silence and respect simply by its nature and atmosphere.

The "Puig" (the word is Catalan for an isolated hill) had been built in 1348 as a place of escape from the Black Death. In 1370 a religious community of nuns moved in, and in 1389 it was established as a monastery. For six centuries both nuns and hermits lived there, until in 1988 the community was finally disbanded and the care of the monastery was taken over by the church administration and a local family.

We stayed for ages admiring the views, which were quite spectacular. You can see from the northern coastline of Cala Sant Vincent to Alcudia and La Pobla and right across to the Formentor headline. On the opposite

Chapter 5

side are the magnificent Tramuntana mountains, where in the summer months the sky turns a deep purple as the sun sets behind them. I had never seen such scenery before at such high altitude.

We visited the adjoining chapel, where a statue of the Madonna and Child presided at the altar, surrounded by hundreds of candles which had been placed there by travellers who had come to pay homage to the religious figures. I noticed an extraordinary energy about the place, and felt something was urging me to make sure I came back. I noticed that there were rooms where you could stay, and knew that I would be returning.

The holiday was over all too soon, and it was back to reality with a bang. At home I was once again plunged into the isolation and abandonment I had been feeling at work. I dreaded going in each day. The feeling of being totally unsupported both at home and at work held me back. I didn't want much – just a normal environment around me, with kind, friendly people.

The spiritualist church continued to be a great comfort to me. Just to be in the company of decent, friendly people made a huge difference to the way I felt on a day-to-day basis. Having that kind of support earlier would certainly have speeded up my recovery.

I was beginning to realise that this was how people should be. Years of living in a family who could not give me the support I needed had brainwashed me into thinking that the situation at home was normal. The constant messages I received in the church confirmed that it wasn't.

One particular message I received really stood out. It told me that unsympathetic people had "pecked my eyes out" with all their negative comments and actions, and now they wanted the very sockets of them – horrific! The medium shook his head in horror. That experience stuck with me for a long time. It confirmed just how bad a time I was having and how deeply people's actions could affect you mentally and physically.

To help my recovery, I began to attend a workmate's home to receive

Chapter 5

Reiki treatment, a form of spiritual healing. Slowly but surely I found I could begin to relax, instead of being a jumbled mess all the time. I also began to feel more centred and stronger in my own identity.

Each week I would feel the layers of stress and anguish within my body drift away. I enjoyed it so much that I decided to learn Reiki and undertook levels 1 and 2, which enabled me to send and receive the healing to myself and others.

At work, I noticed a huge difference when handling babies. Little ones who wouldn't settle for other colleagues seemed to feel my relaxing "vibes" and would settle within minutes in my arms.

The presence I had felt at my mum's house never left me. If anything, now that I was living alone, it began to intensify. It was as if it had stepped up a gear in response to the troubles and loneliness I was experiencing.

Things began to happen to me, usually when I just about to drop off to sleep. I would feel a force around my body. To begin with it never lasted more than a few seconds, but it was enough to jolt me out of going to sleep.

I wondered what was going on. It wasn't a dream, as it would jolt me wide awake. The force was always calm and controlled, but gradually it began to become stronger. At first it frightened me, but the more I relaxed and let it happen, the more the feeling intensified. Little did I know it at the time, but this force was about to take on a life of its own and introduce itself properly to me.

Chapter 6

The Puig

I was back at the Santuario del Puig de Maria within three months of our holiday. That September I booked to go alone, and arranged to stay there. Nothing could have prepared me for what would happen while I was there.

I took a taxi from the airport to Pollensa and from there I made the journey up the mountain on foot. The journey was not helped by the weight of my rucksack and the heat of the midday sun, but I managed it eventually, after stopping a few times to get my breath.

"Reception" was a little hatch in the middle of the door. I rang the bell. The woman who responded spoke some English, which was lucky as I certainly didn't speak any Spanish. She showed me to my 'cell' or celda, as small rooms of this kind are known in Spanish. The cost was a princely £4 a night and I paid up front for my two-week stay. The room was basic, as you'd expect at that price, but it had twin beds and a cabinet on each side. Brown tiles covered the floor and there was a wooden chair in the corner. Old pictures of Jesus and the Madonna and Child hung on the walls.

I opened the shutters to reveal a glorious view. Far below, the old town of Pollensa looked tiny. You could see right across to Port Pollensa and the north coast.

I changed into cooler clothing and set off to explore the Puig and the gardens which surrounded it. It was quite busy with people coming and going from their rooms – not just single people like me but families and couples staying, which was comforting, as I felt a little more relaxed about being on my own. As time went by I was to find that there were many monasteries on the island, the most famous being that at Luc. The

Chapter 6

monasteries are very popular with cyclists who travel from one to another to explore the island - great if money's tight, and a nice contrast to a beach-based holiday.

The gardens were on different levels. The top one was a grassed area with picnic tables and stone barbecues for everyone to enjoy. I imagined how lovely it would be to have a barbecue going and enjoy a cool glass of wine while looking out over the miles and miles of mountains and coastline.

A few tourists were dotted around the picnic area, taking photographs or having a well-earned drink after making the climb. The level below was mostly rocky, with the odd bell-ringing goat munching away at the vegetation. I sat on a large rock hidden away from the tourists at the front of the Puig and overlooking the coast. It was so peaceful, with only the sound of the trees swaying in the wind and a sprinkling of birdsong. Here I would get all the serenity and peace I wanted.

I read some of my book and then strolled back to my room, stopping off at the chapel on the way. The building was cool and serene and the lighting subdued. The doors had been left open and only a brown velvet curtain sheltered the doorway from the sunlight. It allowed a cooling breeze to enter.

At suppertime I went down to the dining room, which was a little room capable of taking perhaps 15 diners. The food was delicious, and so cheap compared to England. Afterwards I took a beer and sat on the stone wall outside, admiring the sunset over the mountains. The air was warm and I could catch the aroma of the pine trees which dotted the mountain landscape.

That night I slept like an angel. The travelling, the sun and the mountain air had made me very tired, and more relaxed than I had been for a very long time. Apart from the sound of my fellow guests returning from the restaurant, it was wonderfully quiet.

Since I had begun my Reiki treatments back home I was beginning to see colours around me at night - apparently this is not unusual when you

Chapter 6

start Reiki. I would see beautiful blobs of green and blue, usually ending with an intense purple. They seemed to emanate above me and would appear to pass into my body. Now that I was at the sanctuary the colours were becoming deeper, bigger and more vivid.

I was entranced by the colours and the way they seemed to seep into my body. I instinctively knew that they were calming me, repairing the damage I had suffered. I know everyone has this repairing experience when they sleep, but only a handful of us actually see the process. The shapes and colours reminded me of the Windows visualisations that show on your computer when playing music, colours that form, twist, drift and morph from colour to colour before your eyes. I drifted off peacefully to sleep.

I woke the next morning feeling very refreshed. The restaurant was closed on a Monday, so I decided to walk down to Pollensa and take the bus to the beach before buying some food on the way back.

After coffee I made my way down the mountain. It was much quicker going down than up - 30 minutes, rather than an hour - but it still made my legs ache.

When I got to Pollensa I decided to stop for a coffee in the main square. I watched the smartly-dressed professionals going about their business, and the women with their designer glasses and dripping gold necklaces sipping their lattes at the more affluent bars in the square. Retired Spanish men sat on their bar stools taking in the scene. No doubt they were paying a lot less for their drinks than the tourists.

The town was very pretty, with breezy cobbled streets, stone architecture and houses painted in an array of Mediterranean colours. The shops were mainly boutiques and florists, with the odd estate agency. There were plenty of quiet areas with benches, trees and water features to encourage a more relaxing and slower way of life. It was all very different from home.

Chapter 6

When I got to Port Pollensa I made my way to a quiet spot on the beach. It was a glorious day and the sun was beating down. I could see fishing boats in the bay, and there were one or two windsurfers practising their skills.

I settled myself down on the sand next to a windsurfing shack, and watched as families got kitted out and received instruction. It all looked rather challenging to me, but I could imagine that once you tried it you could easily get hooked.

I couldn't help noticing that the instructor, who was obviously English, was rather attractive. In particular, he had a very pleasant voice. He had a confidence and an assurance in his voice that made me want to sit up and listen. He noticed me staring at him, which was a little embarrassing, but it was fun to catch his eye and brightened the day up even further. It was a long time since I had felt drawn to a man's company – I must have been getting better! I stayed for a while and then left. I needed to leave in plenty of time to get my bus, buy the food I needed and climb back up to the Puig before darkness fell.

With my shopping in hand, I made my way back up to the sanctuary. The climb seemed to be getting harder, and I found myself wondering why I was punishing myself by doing it again. But at least it was keeping me fit.

I was exhausted when I eventually got back to my room and collapsed on to the bed to recuperate. I decided to go to bed straight after supper, and stopped to watch the sunset again before bed.

On the way I stopped off in the chapel to enjoy the peace and quiet. More candles had been lit and there were fresh flowers around the altar. I had begun to notice that the more time I spent there, the more aware I became of the energy around me. It seemed to be drawing me in, relaxing and calming me, while at the same time it was sharpening my awareness of the religious dimension of the sanctuary. Every time I left the chapel I seemed to feel a heaviness inside my head – not an unpleasant feeling, just a sense that something very powerful was coming from the walls. It

Chapter 6

didn't frighten me, but it did make me feel a deep respect for the place.

That night in bed, the colours came thick and fast. They were so vivid that I simply lay there mesmerised.

I also began to notice that they were now accompanied by what appeared to be sparks of electricity. At first I would see a round silver shape with sparks around it, which then drifted away and became smaller. The experience lasted perhaps five minutes.

The next morning, after coffee and a few chapters from my book, I decided to go back to the beach at Port Pollensa. I couldn't help thinking that it would be nice to see the hunky windsurfing instructor again. I caught the eleven o'clock bus from the town, bought some cigarettes, a drink and a sandwich, and headed for the beach.

I laid out my towel, put on some suntan lotion and settled down to admire the view. Naturally, I made sure it included the instructor! Our eyes kept meeting, but I think after a while he must have got bored with all the staring and disappeared off with a mate of his. "Curiosity killed the cat," I thought. On the bus back I could see the mountain and the Puig, and it looked magical, like a little castle perched up there on the mountain a thousand feet above.

As I set off on my trek up the mountain I noticed the man who ran the Puig speeding down to collect provisions for the following day. The route looked pretty hair-raising to me, but he was clearly used to the cobbles and the tight corners.

The family always looked after me when I went to order my meals, perhaps because I was on my own. There would be two women in the kitchen preparing and cooking the food to order, sometimes under extreme pressure if large Spanish families descended on the little restaurant. Some of them were just visiting for the food and the views. But I was always served on time, and no-one seemed to be deterred by the language barrier. If I couldn't explain what I wanted I would just point to

Chapter 6

the menu. We used to laugh about it, but we always understood one another. They were such a lovely family, always friendly and polite and so gracious and humble even when they had to deal with the most demanding customers. Some of the customers would give them a hard time if they felt their food was a little slow arriving, though they could see that the staff were running frantically round trying to attend to everyone's requirements. I felt like telling them to back off.

That night as I lay in bed drifting off to sleep, my colours came back with an even greater intensity. Then I started to get the 'force' feeling I was familiar with from back home. It felt stronger and more intense. I tried to relax and drift off to sleep, but it came back more powerfully than ever. I had now become more deeply relaxed, which I felt made it easier for it to happen.

I was almost going off to sleep when gently, yet very forcefully, I found myself lifted up and carried away. The next thing I knew I was travelling down some kind of tunnel at what seemed an incredible speed – I could actually feel my hair being blown from my face. I certainly wasn't asleep. I could feel my heart racing as I tried to work out what on earth could be happening to me.

A brilliant spark of light seemed to be accompanying me down the tunnel. I knew I was going somewhere, but I had no idea where, or how and I couldn't stop it.

Then it clicked. I must have died! What other explanation could there be? I'd read about the countless people who had had similar experiences of entering a tunnel of light – near-death experiences.

However, apart from the brilliant point of light accompanying me, there was no light to speak of, no music or angels accompanying me on my journey – quite disappointing! And then I wondered how I could possibly have died – I had been feeling perfectly well and hadn't eaten anything dodgy. The chicken I'd had for supper hadn't been undercooked – if anything it was a bit overdone!

Chapter 6

As these thoughts wandered through my mind, I continued to shoot at the speed of light down the tunnel. The force that was propelling me was enormous. It felt as if I was in the presence of something very big indeed. My hair was still blowing behind me and the speed of it all began to make my stomach turn.

My breakneck journey ended as quickly as it had begun. I stopped, at the end of this strange tunnel, in complete darkness. But I felt quite safe. I stood there waiting for something to happen, but there was complete silence.

Then, quite suddenly, I heard a man's voice. I couldn't see him, but his words were crystal clear. He spoke in a very matter-of-fact, almost critical way, asking me whether my journeys up and down the mountain had been worth it. This made me a feel a little foolish. Somebody - or something - had been aware of my every move and knew that I had made those trips to catch the eye of some bloke on the beach! I was dumbfounded.

The voice then spoke of my gift of mediumship, as if he was confirming this for me. He also told me to write all my experiences down.

I didn't say a word. Although I couldn't see the owner of the voice, I got the impression that he was someone who had lived many centuries ago and was a very wise man with a lot of knowledge to impart. The conviction and strength he spoke with would have stopped most people in their tracks. It was as if he was commanding you to listen.

That was it – there was no further conversation. I felt the force around me begin to disappear, and lay there in my bed waiting for it to go, my eyes completely open.

At last the force disappeared, and I jumped straight out of bed and said out loud 'What the bloody hell was that?' It had shocked me beyond belief. I knew I had crossed some sort of void and felt I had been exposed to something like an afterlife or spirit world.

Chapter 6

I didn't sleep well that night. I was in and out of bed most of the night having countless cigarettes, wondering what it was all about and why was it happening to me.

At seven that morning I was up and dressed and waiting for the café to open so I could get myself a strong coffee. I carried it to the front of the Puig and sat down to drink it.

I felt perturbed and fearful about the night's events. I now knew we were not alone and that there was some sort of 'big brother' out there watching over all of us. I sat there on the rock face, thinking of the many things I had done in life and realising that someone out there knew it all. All day I was very much aware of something or somebody with me. As I queued for my food that evening in the restaurant and looked at the people around me eating and laughing, I thought how little they knew of what I had experienced, there within those very walls

As darkness began to fall that evening and I began to wonder what was going to happen that night, I could feel the fear creeping back into me. A storm was beginning to close in, and as I returned to my room I could see flashes of lightning over the sea. I felt as if I was in a Bram Stoker novel, awaiting the return of Dracula! I was terrified. I did not even dare to shut my eyes for fear of it all happening again. By the time everyone had turned in you could have heard a pin drop.

I needn't have worried. Nothing alarming happened that night. My colours were there of course, mostly greens and purples, and I knew this was to help me feel calmer.

The next day I awoke feeling much more relaxed. I decided to spend the day at the Puig, reading my books and generally relaxing. There was always somebody to talk to and share holiday stories with. People were mostly passing through, staying a few nights before going on to another monastery.

On the way to bed I stopped off at the chapel as usual. Again I noticed the energy and atmosphere, which definitely had more intensity to it that

Chapter 6

evening, so much so that I had to go for a short walk outside to ground myself. It was almost as if the energy within the chapel put you into a meditative state.

I felt relaxed as I got into bed that evening. I read for a while by candlelight and then settled down to sleep. The colours came as usual and I soon nodded off.

I awoke at about four in the morning, feeling rather tearful and despondent. I reflected how gullible I had been with my ex. I started feeling quite sorry for myself and had a little cry. As I settled off I began to see again the silver sparks of light appearing before my eyes. I lay there and watched them, not feeling afraid at all. I remember dreaming a little - and then all of a sudden I was off speeding down the tunnel again as I had two nights before.

Everything seemed much clearer this time and I felt less afraid. Again I was being accompanied by a bright light. This time, when we stopped at the end of the tunnel, a reel of film began to play. It appeared to be some sort of cartoon. The colours were amazing, and the scene was extraordinarily real.

The next morning I got up and began to make my way to reception for my early morning coffee. Normally I would pack my bag with books, a towel and money so I didn't have to return to my room during the day, but as I left my room I heard what sounded like the voice of the man that had visited me at the end of the tunnel.

"Aren't you forgetting something?" he asked. His voice was clear as a bell, yet of course no one was in the room with me. It stopped me in my tracks.

I checked my bag, and sure enough I had forgotten to put my towel in. I felt a little self conscious as I picked up my towel and made my way to the door. Someone knew what I was doing! "Thanks" I said to no-one in a feeble voice. I could have become quite paranoid feeling that I was being watched, but for some reason I was taking it all in my stride.

Chapter 6

As the day went by I was aware of something or somebody with me again, like some sort of ethereal presence. It didn't frighten me, but it was a weird sensation knowing I wasn't on my own. Yet I got used to it. I almost felt I had a friend reassuring me. One night I just knew that someone was sitting on the chair in the far corner of my room. This was quite disturbing. I knew someone was there, I just couldn't see them. I even hid under the bedclothes.

My colours now started to become visible in the day, especially in the evenings. I would sit in the gardens as the sun went down watching them emanating from the trees and shrubs around. It was fascinating. I would sit for hours just watching the colours floating around the branches. I knew that I was being shown that every living thing on the planet had energy within it, and the colours were a representation of the energy.

I also began to see colours around other everyday things, such as cars and planes. I distinctly remember looking up at a passing plane one day and asking whether the people on board would be safe. I then saw the plane cloaked all over in green, which I took to mean that all would be well for the passengers.

The night colours were becoming more and more vivid as well, and I was beginning to see what appeared to be black forms or shapes floating above me on the ceiling. It unnerved me at first, but I got used to it.

One afternoon I was sitting outside the chapel when I heard my grandfather's voice. As I started to think about the fact that people don't really go away when they die, he must have read my mind, because I heard him say "Where do you think we are, Timbuk bloody too?" That was exactly his sense of humour, and it made me laugh out loud. If anyone had seen me laughing to myself they would have thought I needed to be carted off in a white van.

I heard my grandfather again only once, on the evening I left for home. I had arrived early at the port and decided to walk along the seafront and grab a bite to eat before taking a taxi to the airport. I found a lovely

Chapter 6

restaurant and chose an outdoor table. As I sat admiring the view a rather fierce-looking waitress came over and asked me to move into the restaurant, saying it was a table for four. I felt very disappointed, as most of the tables were empty. As it happens the couple sitting opposite overheard and invited me to share their table with them. I was delighted to accept. The waitress's face was a picture.

It was at that moment that I heard the voice of my grandfather. "That's one in the eye for her" he said. I smiled and sat down with the couple.

They said they had only just arrived themselves and were keen to talk about the weather and the island. I told them a little about the Puig, and they seemed intrigued by the place and said they would visit. They were such a friendly couple and I will always remember them coming to my aid.

I was sad to leave the island that day. It had been such a special and magical experience. It was the early hours of the morning when I got home, but I couldn't sleep just thinking about it all.

As I drove back from the kennels with Benson the next day I heard my grandma say how much he had missed me. She was right - he went crazy, jumping and whining at the sight of me.

The following evening I went to the Sunday service at the spiritualist church. I was desperate to talk about what had happened to me and wanted to know whether anyone else had had similar experiences.

The church leader didn't seem at all surprised about my experiences, which rather shocked me. She said how pleased she was for me, and that it was the start of my introduction to the spirit world and of my development as a medium. She also said she had experienced something very similar when she had started out on her own journey many years before. I felt relieved that someone understood what I was talking about, and would be there to give me support if I needed it.

That evening I felt there was some sort of presence in the house. Not scary - peaceful and calm, even heavenly. Then as I made my way upstairs

Chapter 6

to bed I noticed a light following me to the left. It followed me into the bedroom, where sparks of light appeared hovering over and around me, each no more than a centimetre across. They seemed to exude a feeling of calm, warmth and safety. Although I had never experienced anything like it before, I knew it was some sort of angelic presence. I had read books about people having angelic encounters in times of trouble, but to experience it yourself is quite amazing.

As I lay there in the dark the sparks seemed to be darting around and above me amid the colours which had also started to appear. As I closed my eyes to try to sleep I saw brilliant white electric sparks before my eyes, large at first, then shrinking away. No sooner had I drifted off than I became aware of being pulled up and carried off by the force I had experienced at the Puig. This time I wasn't going down a tunnel - I was being taken down my own stairs, accompanied again by a brilliant light. It led me to my back door and showed me that it wasn't locked. I came to and made my way down the stairs - and to my amazement the door really was unlocked. I locked it and went back to bed.

It was clear that somebody or something was looking out for me, keeping me safe and protecting me. As time went by I was to experience more incidents like that. I couldn't work out why it was happening to me.

Within a week of getting home I visited Lilian again to have a reading with her and to give her a silver crucifix I had brought her from Majorca. I knew it was really a gift from Spirit thanking her for the work she was doing for them. She was delighted with the gift, but what really struck me was the way she looked at me. She seemed amazed. "Very, very spiritual" she said. I knew what she meant. I had felt this presence around me ever since my experience at the Puig. It almost felt as if I had some godly presence around me. I had the sensation of being lifted slightly off the ground. I remember her saying she could see angels on my shoulder and that there was even a vision of Christ behind me.

Chapter 6

The atmosphere in the house that night felt warm, safe and secure. The silver sparks came back, and so did my colours. But no sooner had I drifted off than I was awoken again by a new experience, a vision of a screen. My name, date of birth, address, the job I did, my likes and dislikes - everything about me was being projected on to a wall.

Spirit was now manifesting itself on a regular basis. There was no rest. Yet I wasn't perturbed by it at all. It all felt completely natural to me, all part of my daily life. I remember thinking that if people knew what was going on they would run a mile. But to me it felt perfectly normal.

I had also begun to hear Spirit as well. At first I thought I was talking to myself. The evidence that I wasn't came to me over Christmas 1999, at my parents' home. I remember sitting quietly in the lounge pondering questions about life and starting to get answers back in what I could only describe as an old English dialect. Although I had never heard it before or read it in any book, I instinctively knew it was a language from centuries ago. The words and the way they were pronounced were completely different from modern English.

That was the turning point for me, because there was no way on God's earth I could have dreamed that, or made it up. I had also begun to notice that some of the many questions I was putting were getting answers I would never have thought of or known about. That's when I really began to believe that I was indeed able to communicate with the spirit world.

Over the years I continued to receive information that I could not have known in any normal way. Spirit told me I was pregnant, long before I had any symptoms. Another time I had a warning that my son's seatbelt was not fastened – I stopped the car and found that it was true.

These messages were not voices, not something you could actually hear. It was more like someone putting thoughts or ideas into your mind. We have all had these at some time or another, and while you may think they are of your own making, often they may be Spirit helping and guiding you

Chapter 6

through your journey of life. You may also get the impression that you hear a deceased person's tone of voice and personality behind the thoughts. This is obviously how mediums are able to match a person's character to the family or a friend in the audience.

However, some mediums are able to hear 'direct voice' from Spirit – clairaudience, as it's known. Direct voice is exactly what is says - you can actually hear the voice loud and clear. My knowledge of this phenomenon was zero, until I myself experienced it some months following my return from Majorca. I remember waking one morning at around 7 am with someone shouting at full volume down my ear, saying my father was unwell. I knew it wasn't a dream as I had already awoken.

I immediately raced over to my parent's home. I remember greeting my father at the door and asking him if he was ok. He was fine apart, from a slight stomach-ache. It all seemed like a wild goose chase - until about a month later. That's when my father was rushed into hospital with a burst appendix needing emergency surgery.

He had been complaining for months about lower abdominal pain, but it had fallen on deaf ears at home as he was always moaning about stomach upsets. The morning it burst he actually drove himself to hospital.

Chapter 7

A helping hand from Spirit

My mediumship was now beginning to unfold like a flower opening in the sunshine. However, although it had now been some two years since my breakdown, I still had a long way to go in terms of recovery. I was sleeping better, but it was a constant battle to overcome the anxiety and fear. I dreaded the return of the stress I had felt in my head, worse still the possibility of another breakdown. Slowly, over time, my feelings of stress came less and less often, but it would take about five years for them to fade away completely. It was all frustratingly slow and I still often felt in despair.

My immune system took a heavy battering and I was often poorly, with heavy colds, chest infections and water infections. If there was a bug going round, I would catch it. I can understand now why people who live on the breadline or have great stress and worry in their lives succumb more easily to illness and infection. That's what stress does to you - it makes you ill.

Spirit were constantly telling me to slow down and undertake some form of meditation. Often in my sleep I would feel hands on my forehead and know that someone or some 'God' was helping me. My home became a haven of Spirit. I was constantly hearing floorboards creaking, and at night when it was dark I could often make out the outlines of faces floating above me. At first I didn't know who these people were, while at other times I recognised them as my own relatives, particularly my grandma and granddad. I also began to see faces in passing clouds. I would stare for hours at a time to make sure they were really there. I found it fascinating how the faces would change from one person into another. This may all seem a little unbelievable to some, but over the years I have spoken to many people who have had similar experiences, including some of my nursing colleagues. It never surprised me that my colleagues had such

Chapter 7

experiences, as being born healers themselves they would be more susceptible to such phenomena. However I believe anyone can see these things if they take the time to look.

This was proved to me by a lovely lady who tragically lost her baby boy 38 weeks into her pregnancy. It was traumatic for them both, and my heart went out to them. I forged an unforgettable friendship with them, and would often visit regularly just to see how they were getting on. The grief they felt was immense, and I tried as best I could to reassure and support them both.

Then one day I visited them to be greeted by mum with tears in her eyes. She explained to me that she had been to the cemetery earlier in the day to put some flowers and a teddy bear on her little boy's grave when she had looked up to see his face, smiling and chuckling in the clouds. She wept for joy. I was so glad she had seen this as it gave her enormous comfort to know that her little boy was safe, well and looking down on his mummy.

There were times when Spirit would appear while I was dreaming, either to leave a message of reassurance or tell me of something that was going to happen. One night they showed me a dentist's chair. In the morning I awoke with acute toothache, and of course ended up, as they had predicted, at the dentist's having it removed. When I got into bed that night I was in an awful lot of pain, but Spirit came again to bring my healing colours of green and blue.

Looking back I didn't really appreciate the magnitude of what was happening to me, spiritually speaking. All the experiences I was having became normal to me and I imagined they happened to everybody else too. I certainly didn't realise I was being made privy to experiences that even some mediums had never had. I realised this when their reactions revealed that they had never had my experiences.

My neighbour, who was quite a spiritual lady herself, used to say she

Chapter 7

could see sometimes see faces coming through the wall from my house into hers. My sister would also experience spiritual phenomena if we were in contact in the day, and in bed one night she once felt the same force and presence of Spirit I had had. She never really liked it and at times felt quite frightened. In fact she came to dread contact with me for fear of what it would lead to.

But for me it didn't stay within the home. At work I found I could predict when my clients would deliver. Spirit would be in contact with me throughout my working day, helping and guiding me to ensure that births went as smoothly as possible.

One particular experience left me feeling shocked at the power of Spirit. I was working as an on-call community midwife one evening when I had a phone call from a client who thought she had gone into labour. It was her third child, and with the prospect of a rapid delivery I quickly headed over to check her out - she had been booked for a home birth. As I drove I was aware of a tremendous feeling of Spirit - my senses were greatly heightened and I wondered what lay in store.

I arrived at the house to find a relaxed atmosphere and children running about. I did my usual checks; the mother was well, with the baby showing a strong heartbeat and in a good position for delivery. On examination however, I found she hadn't properly begun labour. Normally I would have left her to go into labour naturally and made a follow-up visit a few hours later. However, despite the indications, I had a feeling all was not well. I felt Spirit urging me to send her into hospital. I explained to the mum how I was feeling. She trusted my judgement and we all made our way to the hospital.

When I admitted the lady on to the labour ward I was challenged by the other midwives, who wanted to know why I had brought her in. All I could do was to explain that I had an uneasy feeling about the labour. They must have thought I was mad. They were soon proved wrong. Some

Chapter 7

20 minutes after admission the baby started to show signs of severe distress, with an almost terminal heart trace. The baby had to be delivered quickly and without delay.

The registrar was bleeped. The labour began to advance quickly, and as we waited for the doctor I began to help to deliver it. The head emerged quite quickly, but I then realised to my horror that the shoulders had become completely stuck.

Suddenly I felt Spirit take over my body. I knew it was a man because of the sheer strength. Knowing that time was running out for the baby, I tried again to deliver the rest of the body. As I put my hands either side of the head I suddenly felt two hands being placed on mine and a great force helping me to deliver the child. There were of course no real hands there other than my own. With the help of this new force, I drew the baby safely out. The baby was initially quite poorly, but thankfully it made a complete recovery.

After the delivery I told the midwives what I had experienced, and they seemed as shocked as me, knowing that my instincts had been right. I will never forget that experience as long as I live. It was, quite simply, a miracle.

I was to experience another "helping hand" some two years later while on holiday in the Dominican Republic. On the last day I decided to go white-water rafting. I'd never done it before but I thought I'd give it a go as it seemed fun and adventurous. When we reached our destination we were kitted out in wetsuits and given safety instructions. There were six of us to a boat.

It all started off quite relaxing and peaceful at first, floating down the river as we took in the scenery. There were several different nationalities aboard, and everyone seemed really friendly and was enjoying the ride. However, about a mile downriver the water began to get choppier and the river started to become narrower, with many twists and turns. At first it was exciting, but as the rapids got more turbulent the journey began to

Grandma and Grandpa (Marion and Harold)

Grandma Molly (left) with Grandma Marion, holding me

With Mum and Dad and my sister

On holiday with Mum, my brother and sisters

Aged around 4

With my amazing pal Benson

With Benson on my wedding day in 2005

Looking carefree and relaxed before my whitewater rafting adventure

My graduation ceremony

George with Jacob at the Puig in 2009

On the beach with Jacob, 2009

Mother and son

Chapter 7

become very bumpy indeed. We were eventually all hanging on for dear life, with me, as the smallest, being flung around the boat. Very soon I wanted it all to stop. But it didn't stop; in fact it just kept getting worse. Soon it was so rough that I was barely able to hold on, so numb were my hands from the tension of clinging on.

Just as I thought it couldn't get any worse the speed suddenly increased even further and we hit a rock. I felt myself catapulted into the air. Then, just as I was about to plunge into the water, something or someone literally threw me back into the boat. Nothing was visible - I simply felt a pair of strong hands push me back to safety. After that I was literally sat upon by a very kind German for the rest of the journey to keep me from falling out again.

When we reached the shore I sat there motionless, trying to understand what had happened to me and who or what had saved me. What shocked me the most was the fact that someone was so concerned for my safety. I couldn't understand why.

It was becoming clear that I was being guarded very closely. I remember being told by Spirit at the Puig to write my experiences down on paper, and it was at that point in my holiday when I realised that some day the experience and knowledge I had acquired could be used to reach and support others. My life had a purpose. I just hadn't realised it.

Despite the trauma of the adventure, returning home from that holiday brought me back to earth with a painful bump. My holidays were the only times when I would feel normal and well. It had now been three years since my initial breakdown, and I'd started sleeping better and generally felt better most of the time. However, the reality of re-entering the dog-eat-dog world of work and the realisation that I had very little support always made me feel low and depressed.

Work remained a challenge for me. It wasn't the responsibility or the clients that made my life difficult, but some of the staff I was working with.

Chapter 7

I remember one shift in particular when I was deliberately isolated from company and conversation. It was all down to a couple of them who were out to cause trouble but it hurt like hell, because some of these women had been close friends. They were deliberately trying to hurt me, and all because I wasn't giving them my usual support.

One evening I arrived home feeling particularly low about it all. What had I ever done to anybody? Even my family seemed to have cut me off now that I had found my own place. I felt incredibly lonely and isolated.

That night was probably the worst since my initial breakdown. I felt I had simply had enough of it all. Even the thought of suicide was beginning to creep into my mind. I lay there that night wondering how I might do away with myself. I didn't care about the spiritual experiences I had been having - nothing could help me anymore. I just wanted out.

Then, as I lay there with tears of despair streaming down my face, I began to notice a rising energy within the room. My attention was drawn to the bottom of the bed, where I could see and feel a kind of white mist beginning to encircle my feet. Slowly it began to rise up over my legs until it seemed to be encasing the whole of my body. I felt I was in the presence of something very big indeed. The energy was somehow quite different from anything I had experienced before.

As this extraordinary whiteness began to cover my body, I became aware of the most loving, peaceful energy I had ever experienced. It made me feel safe, secure and hopeful, without a care in the world. The energy was so strong and powerful that I knew I was in the company of God. I felt tiny and humble in His presence. I was given the impression that He was taking care of everything, governing everything in the universe.

It was surreal to be in the company of something so great and holy. It made me forget my sorry, selfish feelings. Now I felt all would be OK, and that I was being kept safe and cared for within the grand scheme of things. It was truly the most amazing experience I had ever had.

Chapter 7

The strange white mist and the energy faded after a couple of minutes, and on waking the next day I just couldn't believe what I had experienced.

Most of the time now I felt more positive about my future, although there were times when I felt I was taking five steps forward and 10 back. There were still more challenges to face and more readjustments to make, especially in terms of having relationships and beginning to trust again. It was all part and parcel of recovering from the trauma of a breakdown. I was still very much in the recovery stage.

My encounter with God was to be repeated one more time, some six months later when I was on a short break in the Lake District. I had spent the day walking with my dog to our favourite place in the mountains near Ambleside. The weather was fine and we were both enjoying the fresh air. We made our way back to the hotel and started to settle down for the night.

This was one of those nights when negative thoughts would creep in while I was on my own. Negativity would soon lead on to fear. I tried to focus on other things, but nothing was working. As I closed my eyes I began to see my silver streaks of energy fading away into a tiny circle as they had done before, and knew that some sort of message was coming my way.

As I dropped off to sleep the force returned. I found myself being carried in someone's arms across what appeared to be a desolate beach. I couldn't see who or what it was, but I knew I was once again in the presence of something very great. It seemed to cradle me. I realised that God was carrying and supporting me in my time of need. I awoke the next day feeling much better.

This made a huge difference to the way I felt about everything. I felt secure and happy, as if someone loved and cared for me after all.

After breakfast I started to head for the mountains again, but on the way I decided to stop at the church. The door was open, so I went in. Nobody was around. I walked along the pews admiring the vastness of the church's interior and the decorated stained-glass windows. As I began

Chapter 7

to leave I stopped at a table by the door to read the various poems on display - poems for the bereaved, for courage, faith, and simply prayers of inspiration. You could buy copies.

I was drawn to one that read 'Footprints'. I had never seen it before, and I began to read it: "One night a man had a dream. He dreamed he was walking along the beach with the Lord..."

As I read the lines I realised I had experienced something very similar the night before. I put some money into the box provided to pay for a copy, and left with it tucked away in my pocket. I still have it, and will always treasure it.

The isolation at the time would have been almost intolerable if it hadn't been for the friendships I had forged at my local spiritualist church. They never judged or abandoned me when I looked worn out, or cried during some of the lovely messages I got during the services. They were always there for me, come rain or shine.

As I was attending regularly I decided to apply for Class B membership, which would enable me to take the accredited Spiritualist National Union healing course. The members gave me their sponsorship signatures and I applied to the Union.

As part of the process of acceptance I had to attend one of the churches in Manchester for an interview about the spiritualist faith and a discussion about the seven principles of spiritualism. I was a little apprehensive about this, but tried to put it to the back of my mind until the day of interview. We were extremely busy at work, so I had very little time for preparation.

I was interviewed by a woman and two men, all in their sixties and smartly dressed. They asked me to introduce myself and talk about the reasons I had chosen to become a member. That part was easy. Then they started to quiz me on the seven principles, but having done little by way of preparation and feeling very nervous, I began to forget and to stumble over my words. Did they really need to ask me all these questions?

Chapter 7

I knew I was a good and sincere person who just wanted to be accepted and further my development. Surely my years of attendance at my church demonstrated my commitment to the faith and the way of life.

As I stumbled on, I could see they weren't impressed. It all seemed very formal and their looks of disapproval were making me extremely uncomfortable.

Then suddenly I began to notice a growing energy behind me. It felt as if someone was wrapping their arms around me. The energy started to rise and rise until I could feel it all around me. I could see from the looks on the interviewers' faces that they could feel it to.

Now it was their turn to become nervous. They began shifting in their seats and looking uncomfortable, in great contrast to their previous behaviour. They became much warmer towards me and started to apologise for making me nervous.

I knew something or someone had been shown to them. It had shown them that I was a good and sincere person and worthy of their acceptance. They approved my membership there and then.

As I drove away I said a silent "thank you" to Spirit for the help I had received.

Chapter 8

Making contact

In March 2001 I made the first of many visits to the famous Arthur Findlay College in Stansted. I had heard about it through my friends at my local spiritualist church and decided to take a trip myself to see what it was all about. The college, originally built in 1871, was given as a gift by Arthur Findlay, a former honorary president of the Spiritualists' National Union to be used in the advancement of spiritualism and psychic sciences. It runs many residential courses where students can strengthen and enhance their mediumistic abilities. It attracts many people from all over the world and is renowned for its teachings in spiritualism and its way of life.

I didn't want to do a course in mediumship, as I didn't feel I had the confidence to stand up in front of groups of people making a complete idiot of myself. Instead I enrolled on a five-day course entitled 'The Rainbow of Life', which covered a variety of topics.

It was with a great sense of excitement that I packed my bags and headed to the station for the five-hour train journey. The house turned out to be magnificent, with beautiful old oak-panelled walls. The library held hundreds of books for all to read, and the grounds were beautifully landscaped. The beautiful calm energy reminded me of the Puig. You knew immediately that there was a great deal of history and religion within those walls.

The course covered meditation, music, colour, art therapy and how to develop and maintain positivity within your life. The tutors and the people I met were friendly and fascinating and we'd all migrate to the bar in the evenings to chat and discuss the day's events.

The people on the course were from all countries and all walks of life.

Chapter 8

Some had travelled from Austria, and one man was from America. He was an older gentleman who had studied paranormal activity all his life and said he was a modern day "ghostbuster". He was fascinating to listen to, and showed us many photos he had taken of ghostly apparitions.

There were no expectations placed upon us to perform any type of mediumship - we were simply expected to enjoy the teachings and relax with like-minded folk. On the last day however, they did ask if anybody would like to try some mediumship. A few of us got up to give it a try. When it was my turn, I immediately got the impression of an elderly lady called Elizabeth who had worked extremely hard in her life and enjoyed baking. I gave a few other details which provoked a response from a lady in the group – she said it must be her grandmother, who had passed over 20 years before. It wasn't an in-depth reading, but at least I had given it a go.

Next up was the paranormal investigator. He had never experienced any form of mediumship himself, so he was very nervous. But no sooner had he got up than he started to give out information about a person who had passed away many years ago. It seemed to roll off his tongue as if he'd been doing it all his life. A woman in the group recognised it as her brother. It was incredible to watch, and I remember feeling really excited for him. I was pleased for him, because he had not thought he had any type of gift. He looked shocked when he had finished, as if he couldn't quite believe he had been able to deliver all this information.

I realised that we must all have this gift to some degree, but most of us are completely unaware of it. Mediumship isn't for some elite group of people; any of us can do it, it's just that some people go on to develop their skills further.

The course helped me learn about the different types and styles of mediumship and the different ways Spirit can communicate with us. I learned how each individual can have one or more skills when working

Chapter 8

with Spirit. Because I was able to hear and feel Spirit around me I was told I had the gifts of clairaudience, to be able to hear those in the spirit world, and clairsentience, meaning to feel and experience them.

An example of clairsentience is being able to feel how the deceased person may have passed away, or what ailments they may have had in their lifetime. The medium actually feels the ailments, so if the person died from, for example, a heart attack, the medium will feel the chest pain. Some mediums are able to see the spirit person or animal in front of them, either as a solid form in front of their eyes or as in a reel of film being played, like watching a television screen. Everyone will experience these things differently, depending how Spirit wishes to work with you.

During my visit I had begun to notice that I would feel a sensation of burning before any demonstration I gave. The tutors explained that this was a normal event when you were just about to connect with the spirit world - it was a result of the energies building between the two sides. It was all new to me, but I was learning fast. I was glad there were people there I could relate to with the experiences I was having.

I left the college feeling renewed and encouraged, knowing that there were others like me who were experiencing similar things and that I wasn't on my own. Above all everyone had been extremely friendly and welcoming, which is what I needed at the time. It was almost a home from home.

The demonstrations that fascinated me the most involved the work of trance medium-ship, which mostly involved the masters within the spirit world coming through the medium and imparting their wisdom and knowledge to the congregation. Sometimes the speakers would give personal readings, but most of the time was taken up with questions from the audience being channelled to the speaker through the medium. Usually the questions would centre on world issues such as war and conflict, with Spirit guiding us on how we should live our lives in

Chapter 8

generating the peace that was needed within the world. It was very interesting stuff, and mind-blowing to listen to.

The evening I returned I had a ticket to see a trance medium demonstration at my spiritualist church, so there was just time to shower and change before going out again. I had seen a couple of demonstrations before, so I had an idea what to expect. I knew that this type of mediumship was reserved for the more experienced medium. It is different because the medium allows himself or herself to be overshadowed by the spirit communicator, allowing the communicator to talk directly through his or her voice. This type of mediumship is usually performed when the medium is partially conscious or in an extremely deep meditative state. It can take many years to reach this level, because surrendering yourself to such an extent takes a great deal of trust and confidence between the medium and Spirit.

The medium was one I hadn't seen before, though I had heard of him on the medium circuit. He came up on to the platform and sat in a huge wooden chair. He was a very upbeat, vibrant person and soon started to get the audience going with the positive energy he had, which would hopefully create the right vibrations for the demonstration. He explained a little about how he worked and said that he would start by getting comfortable in his chair and he would then begin to relax into a deeper state. He asked us to remain quiet.

The hall lights were turned down low, and he began to meditate. You could see him going deeper and deeper within himself. His face and body seemed to relax, so that he looked as if he was asleep.

After a few moments he began to shift about within his chair, and seemed to awake. But by the sound of his voice and the body posture he was adopting you knew it wasn't him at all, but a spirit of some form speaking through him.

The medium began to speak - but not in his own voice. It was slightly deeper in tone and had a German accent. The audience was spellbound.

The Spirit person who was now overshadowing the medium began to welcome the audience. He spoke in a jovial manner. He seemed pleased to be in the company of us all in the congregation.

As he began to speak I immediately knew that he was of master status within the spirit world, and that he had previously been a physician. It was interesting that I was picking all this up, as it hadn't happened to me before at other demonstrations. He confirmed my insight as he went on to explain who he was and when he had lived. He talked of living many lives, and I got the impression that he had lived many centuries ago.

Then he invited questions from the audience. I can't remember the questions, but I do remember him asking to come to me. I always got nervous when approached by the mediums and often wished they would choose somebody else, but that night, knowing he was a master, I took a nervous gulp before he even began to speak to me.

I very humbly said hello, and awaited his message. Suddenly a new voice seemed to emerge from the medium's mouth. He had taken on the voice of an elderly woman who introduced herself as Rose. She sounded shy. She began by telling me I had seen and heard Spirit as a child, but that it had lain dormant after my childhood years. I took it that my spiritual abilities had been suppressed by the parenting and influences I had received.

She explained that I had been given a second chance as a rebirth in this lifetime, but that I had in fact been working for Spirit all my life. My purpose within this lifetime was to heal, and to impart the knowledge I had learned to others.

It was a pivotal moment for me, as I had not known I had had this ability as a young child, or that it had been lost. I thanked the lady for her words of inspiration and with that she moved on to someone else. A few further readings were given and then came the finale to the service. The

Chapter 8

physician came back through the medium and we began to listen to some words of wisdom from the masters themselves.

The physician began to explain that the millennium had brought with it a great change in consciousness for everyone. A spiritual shift had occurred, with people gaining an increased understanding of everything around them - a deepened level, so to speak. However, the world was still experiencing war and strife and that much more would have to be done if things were to improve.

They said 'great discussions' were going on as to how this could be achieved, and that as a result we would experience more natural disasters, which would bring about an increased understanding and an alignment to a more god-like consciousness - a spiritual awakening. They talked about needing 'more workers in the vineyard', meaning they wanted more people to join forces around the world in disseminating peace and light towards others to increase their spiritual consciousness. It was amazing to listen to and although they gave the impression that they didn't have all the answers, something within me knew that everything was being formed as it should be and moving forward in the right direction.

After about 10 minutes the energy began to fade and the physician said how good it had been to talk to the congregation. He wished everyone a very good evening, and with that he was gone.

Everyone watched as the medium regained his own personality and came out of his meditation. You could tell he was coming back by the way his face started to relax. He began to shift in his chair and his eyes began to open. Once he appeared more alert, he asked if it had been a good demonstration. He had no idea what had been said. His assistant told him it had, and removed the cassette from the tape recorder - a recording had been done of the demonstration.

It was spellbinding stuff to listen to. You knew from what had been said that they meant business. Strangely, I remember thinking how awful

Chapter 8

it was that others were to suffer in natural disasters. I had begun to understand however that people really only learn and grow spiritually through the pain and difficulties that life throws at them. Despite understanding this, I still wrestle with it, simply because I don't like the thought of anyone suffering.

Something strange happened to me that evening. Not only was I given a message, but during the service I had started to receive thought impressions of who the gentleman was who spoke to us through the medium. I had known his age, his job and what level of spiritual plane he was on before he had told us himself. This had never happened before.

As the last few messages were given out I had also begun to gain an awareness of the differing levels and realms within the spirit world that we all go to on our passing. The information came thick and fast. They made me aware that when they pass on, most good honest people enter at levels 3 and 4, depending on the spiritual progression they had gone through before passing. Simply put, the better the person, the higher the level they will transcend to.

They explained that the higher realms were for those who have lived many lives with much experience behind them, and as a result had attained a purer, near-godlike state of consciousness, the masters of the spirit world. Information came through to me about the lower realms and how these were reserved for the lower kind of people – those who are deceitful or evil, such as rapists and murderers. Level one was the worst of all.

I was left with the impression that everything is taken care according to the life or lives you have led and whether or not you have dealt well with the challenges and lessons life has given you.

I left the church that evening mulling over what had been said and thinking about the spiritual shift that had occurred around the millennium. I had begun to notice the changes myself, especially the

Chapter 8

growing interest in healing therapies such as reflexology, aromatherapy and Reiki spiritual healing. It seemed that suddenly hundreds of people had turned to administering these therapies, either going private or opening their own business establishments to practise their healing. Since the millennium I had also begun to notice more discussions and demonstrations taking place of a spiritual nature, especially through the media. More films seemed to portray the afterlife or contain a spiritual element, such as The Green Mile, The Perfect Storm, The Sixth Sense and most recently The Lovely Bones. I had also begun to notice that around the millennium the birds had begun to act a little strangely by singing sometimes until three in the morning. I remember going to work one morning and commenting on this to a colleague, who had also noticed it.

It was all rather odd. I knew something was shifting and changing for all of us, and it was doing so on a grand scale.

That night after the demonstration I started to think about the differing spiritual realms, especially the lower realms, thinking what an awful place it must be and how important it was to try and be a good person within your lifetime. I didn't really have any idea what they might feel or look like. Little did I know as I settled off to sleep that night that I was about to find out.

Chapter 9

Positive and negative

I settled off to sleep on the night of the demonstration with no idea of what I was about to be shown by the spirit world. It wasn't a nice experience, but I believe I should share it. I knew at the time that I would be writing about my experiences, as I believe Spirit showed me so that I could show others what happens if you live a life that strays too far from the path of good.

I have learned that it's true what they say – "what goes around comes around", once we have passed over. Everything you do is logged in the spirit world on a day-to-day basis throughout your life. Every word or deed, good or bad, is recorded - you can't hide. It is your responsibility and no-one else's to make sure your behaviour is as good and honest as possible. It's as simple as that.

Of course, we all make mistakes – it's human nature - but it is how we learn and change for the better that really makes the difference, especially if we can help others along the way too.

If you have suffered at the hands of another, you may feel they haven't had their 'comeuppance' for what they did. I can assure you they will eventually. Some of us may find this comforting. It must be especially difficult for families who have experienced the trauma of losing a loved one through the deliberate evil acts of others. I often think about poor Keith Bennett, the boy whose life was taken by the Moors Murderers. I can only try to imagine what that family, especially Keith's mother, have gone through. Tragically, she is not alone. The devastation such people are left with is unimaginable. Some may find a way to forgive, but they could never forget.

As I drifted off to sleep that night I was made aware of the force-like

Chapter 9

feeling around my body once more. For once I wasn't that keen on receiving any more information from Spirit. Not only was I tired, but the force was much more powerful than normal, which made me wonder what I was about to be shown.

I was given no choice. The force overpowered my body and I felt myself dropped into what I can only describe as a dungeon. I had to stand and watch what was happening. It was no dream. I felt fully awake, but unable to stop what was happening.

The room was large, with other rooms leading off it. It was dark, though there was enough light to allow me to see what was going on. I felt evil black energies within the room and around me. I could make out beings squirming around on the floor, screaming and screeching in turmoil and pain. I couldn't see their faces, but they seemed to be hideous and non-human. Some of them had blood dripping from their mouths. The walls were stained with blood.

It was absolutely terrifying. All I wanted to do was to get out of there and wake up, but I couldn't. They wouldn't let me. I screamed and pleaded with Spirit to release me, but they were keeping me there to experience it first hand.

Eventually, after a few moments, they let me go. I woke up screaming the place down. I have never been so terrified in all my life. My heart was racing and I was sweating with fear. It took me a few moments to catch my breath.

When you have a nightmare, you can at least console yourself with the knowledge that it wasn't real. This was only too real. I couldn't believe what I had been shown - it was the worst thing I had ever experienced.

It took me at least an hour to summon up the courage to get out of bed. I thought something would be on the landing, waiting to get me. I was too shocked and frightened to sleep at all that night.

What was most difficult about that experience was the fact that up until

Chapter 9

now I had been helped and supported by Spirit. This was very different. I had learned that in the spirit world as in our own, not everything in the garden is rosy.

Spirit wanted me to spread this message. They wanted me to tell the world how important it is for people to recognise the consequences of their actions in this life. I personally don't believe there is a hell, although the place I went to certainly felt like hell. I believe we make our own hell here on earth. Hell to me is hatred, negativity, deceitful and evil acts by others. When we behave this way we are descending to a lower level of being, with very little to offer the world but pain and suffering to others.

If you are a good and honest person you'll know when you come into contact with others who don't operate like you. Through their own insecurities (which are usually due to a lack of confidence and esteem within themselves) they will immediately see you as a threat and try to drain you of all your positive energy. We all sense this from people from time to time.

Unfortunately people like this contaminate the rest of us. They make you feel bad about yourself and they'll soon have you questioning your own behaviour. Countless times I have heard people say, "Is it me? Am I being silly?" The answer is, no – people like this just make you feel that way. They will wreck your confidence. There's only one answer – stay away from them.

Yet such people always seem very sad to me. Deep down they are crying out for some kind of love and reassurance. They may never admit to this, even to themselves, but is true. You can always trace it back to some kind of ill treatment in their younger years which has given them a deep sense of insecurity.

Learning how disciplined and strict the spirit world could be was hard for me. I discovered that excuses weren't allowed. Everything was very much black and white – you are either good or bad, with no in between.

Chapter 9

Probably because I had undergone so much unpleasantness myself, I thought the spirit world was all about inflicting bad situations on to us. I know now that this is not so. You are responsible for your own actions. If you send out negative energy to others, you will receive negativity back. If you send positive energy, or at least try to, you will be putting the right signals out and receiving the positive energy back. It's as simple as that.

I had to learn all this as part of my own journey of self-improvement. On reflection, it was a lesson which had been lined up for me. Until I had my breakdown I had never been a negative person. I had tended to be very positive in my life and had many riches as a result - I had a good social life, work had always gone well and although my family weren't as supportive in my life as they could have been I continued to remain positive within my life. My breakdown and the problems I had had with my husband had tarnished some of the goodness and positivity.

It was now three years since the breakdown, and I was still finding life a struggle. Although the dark stress in my head had begun to subside I still found I had to battle with the constant anxiety and stress of ordinary daily life. Life was bad enough without having the after-effects of mental illness to contend with. Life seemed to be a constant struggle, and it was very hard to stay positive.

I know now that I needed to experience some real negativity, and that it was just part of my life's plan to experience it first hand. I believe it was a lesson designed to show me how real people feel at times. In hindsight it has made me into a better nurse and a better citizen, as I can now relate to some of the pain and grief people have to endure.

In April 2001 I began to experience the full reality of what my nervous breakdown had done to me. My work, my friendships, my social life and the dynamics of my family had all been adversely affected. Sometimes everything seemed a total mess. Work was a nightmare – colleagues I had regarded as friends were treating me like something they'd scraped off

Chapter 9

their shoes. Other so-called friends had long disappeared from my world.

At home, my family were still entertaining my ex-husband, and I had found out that he was even babysitting my sister's children. It was unbelievable. I felt isolated and lonely. It looked as if my life would never get back on track. The experiences I was having were beginning to leave me feeling alienated from others around me.

I began to wonder why other people weren't suffering like me, especially those who seemed to care nothing for others. I began to think that the nastier you were the more you were respected. I was working with people who seemed to me to be sailing through life as if it was all one big party. They seemed to get promotion after promotion. They would end up as the most terrible leaders or managers, but everyone seemed to like them. It was infuriating that nobody seemed to notice their flaws. The real gems, the true leaders, never got a chance because they wouldn't push and shove like the others to get to the top.

I felt angry that I had suffered such hardships while others seemed to be having an easy ride of it all. It didn't seem fair that some idiot - my ex - had come into my life, dumped a load of his emotional rubbish on to me and left me burdened with it. His baggage had become my baggage, and I felt I had let it happen.

I remember writing an angry letter to him saying how he had made me feel and how his behaviour had affected my life. He just used it as a ploy to get closer to my family. I found this out because my older sister told me it was a horrible letter and should never have been written!

They were difficult days. No-one seemed to understand how I felt. The negativity began to grow within me and I felt I hated everything and everyone. I would take long walks with my dog to try to feel better about everything. I would usually end up marching along in a fury ranting to myself.

"Why me?" I would ask. And the answer I got back from Spirit was

Chapter 9

always "Why not?" I found this very annoying. Even my house no longer felt like a safe haven; there seemed to be something dark and negative within its walls.

What I didn't realise was that this negativity was attracting unwanted visitations by certain lower-realm spirits into my home. One morning at around 6 am I woke to realise that someone or something was standing beside my bed. I felt uneasy and kept my eyes closed in the hope that it would go away. I waited several minutes, but it would not go away. In the end I plucked up the courage to reach out a hand to see if there was anything there. Immediately I felt a hand. That was something I had never experienced before. It seemed to be a real hand, fleshy, neither warm nor cold. There was just one odd thing about it – the hand had only three fingers.

When I realised that I immediately let go. I opened my eyes to see a black figure in front of me. Although I couldn't see its face, I instinctively knew it was a woman. She had a small stature with curved shoulders. She appeared to be wearing a black robe.

I knew she was not a good spirit. She seemed to exude a devious, sly nature. Neither of us spoke. After a few moments she disappeared, and I can't begin to say what a relief it was. I had been frozen with fear.

This was a first for me, as I had never properly seen any type of spirit before, good or bad let alone felt them physically.

I got out of bed and got dressed. I needed to speak with my medium friend Lilian about what I had just experienced, to get her support and reassurance. When I rang her she agreed to see me that morning. I think she realised how urgent it was.

I arrived at Lilian's place in quite a state. As she started to give me a reading she suddenly looked over my shoulder. She said she had seen an old lady in Victorian clothes. This, she said, was the woman who had visited me.

Chapter 9

Lilian said this woman had not been a good character in her past life and for some reason she had latched on to me because I had had some connection with her. She thought it might have been work related, as I had apparently worked as a nurse at that time, helping to fight for better working conditions.

Then Lilian said she could see the woman touching my car keys and other property from my handbag. She told her to leave them alone. She then very politely asked her to leave me and my home, and we both said a prayer for her.

Almost immediately I felt like the atmosphere lift. "I think she may have gone," she said. I let out a huge sigh of relief, and started wondering what it was all about. Had I done something wrong? Why had she been attracted to me?

Lilian said the woman had been with me at my home for some time. I told her the atmosphere had seemed very dense and heavy lately, but I hadn't been able to put my finger on a reason.

Lilian said I had attracted this woman because of the way I had been feeling. She had liked the dull energy I had been unknowingly emitting because it was similar to hers. I had unknowingly been welcoming unwanted spirit visitors into my life and my home. If I had known this I would have tried harder to "think positive". She explained that not everything connected with the spiritual side of life is rosy and nice. Anyone getting involved in the spiritual side should be aware that there is another side to the coin.

She added that she was being told by Spirit that I was meant to experience this, as it would help to prepare me for my future work. She also said how important it was now for me to shut myself off to Spirit, just to give myself a breather and stay protected. For the sake of my own health, it was now becoming necessary to break that link some of the time. I was becoming depleted of my own energies.

I understood what she meant, but I didn't know how to do this, so she

Chapter 9

spent the rest of the morning demonstrating exercises to help me break off the link. She talked through the different locations of the chakras within the body and spoke of imagining closing a door or a flower, starting from the crown of your head and finishing at your feet. Then when I was ready to work with Spirit again I should imagine the flowers or the doors opening over each chakra.

I was very glad I had Lilian to advise and support me. Now that more and more people are attending the spiritualist churches, there is always someone who can help and advise you when you need it. Many choose to attend the awareness classes that are held there, which will introduce you to such exercises. I did some classes myself but found it just wasn't for me as at the time I was just too shy and nervous of other people. Lilian spoke about me having my own circle of spiritual support around me all the time, as Spirit was always helping and guiding me in my daily life. In truth I found it difficult to mix at the churches because of the trauma I had experienced. I felt no-one could have related to how I was feeling. I was just too raw. I was still getting over the physical and emotional effects of my breakdown. That's why my development was done in private. I would mentally ask questions about life and its challenges, and answers would always come.

Lilian had given me lots of food for thought concerning the importance of thinking positive within your daily life. That day she talked about how important it was to send positive thoughts out in your everyday life. She said negative thought only serves to draw negativity to us, so we tend to live a miserable life. It can all become a vicious circle.

Staying positive is much easier to talk about than it is to do. More and more books are being published on the subject, most of them claiming it's as easy as 123 and that once you've read the book your problems will be over. The truth is that some people will always have to face hard challenges in life, often through no fault of their own. It's easy for people who don't

Chapter 9

have a care in the world to talk about positivity. It's a different matter for someone who is penniless, homeless and jobless! Spiritual philosophers would argue that money shouldn't really come into it, but unless you've been there you cannot really know what it feels like for others.

Many people feel guilty about feeling sad, negative or depressed, because our society dictates that it is socially unacceptable. This is nonsense. Such feelings are part of life and part of human nature. Without the negative side we could not really experience and appreciate joy in our lives.

Spirit has always told me never to worry about the way I feel - just acknowledge it and tell yourself that it will pass. It is part and parcel of who you are, and a normal response to some of life's stresses and strains. In fact it helps us to better ourselves in the long run. At the same time, being constantly negative will win you no friends. In today's society it would seem some people would rather run a mile than offer a kind word of support. Personally I have always chosen not to walk away. I always try to offer a kind word of support. That's what helps people - not stony silences. You will never know how far a kind word might go in helping others. We all need somebody – and it might be you next time.

Years ago there wasn't as much mental illness and depression as we see today, simply because families were much stronger and members supported each other. Communities too were much closer-knit and your neighbours would usually be only too glad to offer a sympathetic ear and a few words of support. What sort of society have we built where people are found dead after lying undiscovered for weeks because no-one noticed they weren't around? It demonstrates the state of affairs we've all got ourselves into and the society we have created.

Through all my dark times, I knew that eventually something more positive would come out of it all. Although there were times I would curse God because I felt so abandoned, I managed to stay on track. I recall one

Chapter 9

night asking Spirit why I was experiencing such bad luck. They began to play a film showing me a corridor with rows of portraits on the wall. "Many people have gone before you," they said. "It is your life purpose to work for Spirit'. Spirit would explain to me that I needed experience and knowledge to be more effective in my work with them, a more empathetic person, someone who would truly be able to relate to others.

At other times they would argue with me, saying it was I who had chosen to undergo the experiences and explaining that before our earthly life begins we decide what experiences we will undertake within our lives in order to grow, learn and become more spiritual. I used to think I would hardly have signed up for a nervous breakdown, but they would simply reiterate that we lose the memory of it when we pass over to the earthly life. They would say that we have all had many lives before, perhaps hundreds, so that we may accumulate experience and knowledge which will in turn escalate us to a higher spiritual level when we pass over.

I truly believe now that the more pain you suffer, the higher the rewards will be for you when you return to the spiritual realms and the God force that governs us all. No pain, no gain, if you like.

So with the experiences of the lower realms behind me, and feeling I had a better understanding about the need to keep positive in my life, I began to spiritually shut myself down as I embarked on a more disciplined and healthier way of life.

.

Chapter 10

Escaping from the past

As 2001 went on I began to feel that the mental fog I had been feeling for so long was at last beginning to lift. Until then the sheer stress of everything I had been through had prevented me from reflecting fully on how my breakdown had come about. It was now time to start examining what had led to it, to look at the abusive relationship I had got myself into and to see what I could have done to prevent it all happening.

I certainly did not want another relationship like the one I had had and I knew I would never survive another breakdown. After my divorce I did make some mistakes; I would throw myself into relationships to try to make myself feel better. It didn't work, of course. I think that like many people in the aftermath of a broken relationship I went a little wild for a time. However, while I enjoyed the initial high these flings gave me, I was always left feeling low and unloved again as soon as they were over.

Fortunately I began to learn from my experiences, and as I began to recover I made better choices.

To anyone who finds themselves in my position, I would say - give yourself time to recover from the relationship, especially if it was an abusive one. You will need time to recuperate and to feel a healthier person again, mentally and physically. If you have the support of others, accept it and absorb the healing it offers.

You may also have to learn healthier patterns of thinking and behaviour to help you to move forward in your life. Your confidence and self-esteem will have been battered out of you. You may have adopted unhealthy, negative thought processes and started to feel bad about yourself. You will need to take time to examine these issues closely, otherwise you may slip back into the same patterns again.

Chapter 10

The more you can learn to accept and love yourself, corny as it might sound, the better you will be able to protect yourself from others. Being able to love yourself means not only that you will be able to respect others around you - more importantly, you will be able to respect yourself. That in turn will help you to set healthy boundaries around you, which will make it harder for others to harm you and exploit your vulnerability.

You will need to build your confidence and self-esteem to do this. These qualities are the vital building blocks to the success which is out there for the taking and available to everyone. With them, you will be able to say 'no' more easily and you'll find you are able to walk away from an unhealthy situation, whether it is a damaging relationship or a bullying boss.

As I discovered, it takes an enormous amount of courage and strength to walk away from an abusive relationship. Many people find it incredibly difficult to find the necessary strength within them to leave. Anyone who has tried to make an important decision when they were stressed or anxious will know how difficult it is to remain focused and keep a sense of perspective. Others may accept the behaviour, perhaps because they have experienced similar behaviour in childhood. In such cases people may develop a level of tolerance most of us would find hard to understand. Others stay because of the children, or financial considerations.

I used to hear people at work saying "She just brings it on herself because she stays with him". If you have ever been tempted to say that about someone, please remember that you have no idea what that person is going through. Walking away is much, much harder than you realise.

The process of recovery will involve examining your own past and the parental influence and childhood environment you have been exposed to. To protect yourself from ever becoming involved with the wrong kind of partner again, you will first need to make a journey of self-discovery. Leaving an abusive partner is only the first step of your journey.

Many, many positives will come out of this process. You will gain a

Chapter 10

richer way of life, with the possibility of meeting someone who will be a lot more stable and caring in their approach to life. That's what happened to me.

Day by day, month by month, year by year, the mental confusion began to settle. As things became clearer for me and my inner strength increased, I knew it was time for me to deal with some of the experiences I had had with regard to my family. Although I had moved on in my life, with a new home and an amazing promotion at work which put me in charge of the maternity department, I was still being hurt by them because they were still seeing my ex regularly. This was mainly because they were still treating my ex as if nothing had happened. They were totally ignoring what he had done to me. They knew perfectly well that he had sexually and emotionally abused me for years, making me ill to the point of a nervous breakdown. He had taken money from me. Yet they pretended he had done nothing wrong. They were now letting him isolate me from my own family.

I had pleaded with them on countless occasions to cut him off, but it just didn't happen. The pain from this was at times unbearable. It certainly made my recovery much harder. My family had meant everything to me, they were my backbone, but now it had all gone.

I had to walk away from the situation once and for all, not just to recover from him but from them and what they had done to me. Spirit was urging me to do the same. They said I had suffered a life-threatening experience and needed a quiet, healthy environment in which to recuperate.

The crunch came on Christmas Eve 2001, when I visited my sister. I noticed that John's name was there among the place settings for Christmas Day, yet mine was not. I was invited only for Boxing Day.

I spent Christmas Day alone that year. It should have been a happy Christmas – there was snow, for once - but instead I ended the day crawling up into bed with rather too much vodka inside me. The thought of John

Chapter 10

laughing away on such a special day with my family made me want to curl up and die.

After that I vowed to go it alone. I knew I couldn't continue to live with such a situation. But as ever, out of the negative came a positive. It made me examine the reasons why they were ignoring my situation and my feelings. I had begun to unlock the door to the truth within my life and the demons within.

When I look back at my past, I realise that I had what many would class as a privileged upbringing. My parents had started out with nothing, but over the years, through sheer hard graft, they had managed to build an extremely successful business serving the richer areas of Cheshire. Money was never tight, but they quite rightly made sure that none of us took it for granted.

However, although the money they were bringing in provided us with the material necessities of life, I don't ever remember being told I was loved. There were no hugs. I remember craving to be held, to feel wanted. Even as a child I sensed that they had had a harsh upbringing themselves. That made me feel I had to make sure they were ok, especially my mother.

Mum was not an emotionally strong woman. She would cry easily, and I always felt that something very bad must once have happened to her. When she cried, it wasn't just a few passing tears - I could feel the hurt within her. It was as if she couldn't cry for long for fear of the floodgates opening. As we grew up she did admit that she hadn't had much of a childhood and that she had been beaten.

We were not encouraged to show feelings. If something went wrong, from a fall off a bike to a split with a boyfriend, we were just told to get on with it. It was a hard way of life. As time went on I learned never to talk about anything that was affecting me. Our feelings and emotions seemed to be no part of their parental responsibility. I know we were loved, but it was a controlling sort of love. I always felt my oldest sister used to get away with murder, but not the rest of us.

Chapter 10

When Jane and I were born I don't think mum was too pleased, as she hadn't bargained for a set of twins. I will always remember her saying we had been a big mistake. She seemed to enjoy telling us how she cried buckets on hearing she was having twins. I would hear this over and over again. How did she imagine it made us feel?

She would tell us all she'd had enough of us even when we had been good as gold. I don't really think she knew how her behaviour affected us.

As a sensitive child I suffered more than the others and came out of it all with terrible insecurities. I had little self-confidence or self-esteem, and not being allowed to express myself made me very vulnerable as a young adult. I didn't have the confidence to say no to people, and if things were going badly I felt I couldn't say how I felt because I had learned not to.

Perhaps it was because I was used to a controlling environment that I got involved with a man who was a controlling type. When it all went wrong in my marriage, I didn't know how to speak up for myself. In my mind, my feelings just weren't important. That's why, when I eventually did speak out, it was like the lid coming off a pressure cooker.

So after that Christmas I parted company from my family, at least for a time. It was very hard to choose a solitary life over one with a family around me. Hearing John had spent a holiday with my folks made my mind up. I'd challenged them about this at the time, but as usual they didn't want to talk about it or acknowledge my feelings. I wondered once again how this man had got such a hold on my family, despite what he had done to their daughter.

I decided to seek help. I had become braver and stronger now and where once I had been unable to speak about my situation because of stress, I was now beginning slowly but surely to make sense of what had happened to me. I decided to contact my local women's refuge to seek some sort of support and advice.

I knew about the work of these refuges through my experiences with the women I had cared for as a midwife, so I rang the local refuge for advice. I needed to know if I was the only person this had ever happened

Chapter 10

to, especially with regards to my family. The refuge workers were brilliant, as I had felt sure they would be, and I arranged to meet two of them, Sally and Jill. When I pulled up outside the building I saw that it was bristling with CCTV security cameras. It was a huge building, but quite hidden from the road.

It was a shock for me to see the looks on their faces when I told them my story. They were aghast. They couldn't believe the strength I had found to cope with my experiences. Perhaps I myself hadn't realised the sheer enormity of what I had had to endure.

Sally and Jill helped me to offload what had happened to me in a safe and non-judgemental environment. They encouraged me to speak openly, which gave me that all-important permission to talk and to realise that it was OK to do so. They reiterated time and again that it had not been my fault, which in turn helped me to start feeling good about myself again. I had carried all these negative feelings with me since my break-up, reinforced by my family's lack of support. I remember thinking that I must have caused it all myself. No-one had ever said, "It's not your fault, Suzanne!"

The support workers at the refuge took this burden away from me, simply by believing me and telling me it wasn't my fault. It was easy for them to understand, because most of them had been in similar situations themselves. They knew how cunning people like John could be because they had seen it all before. They talked about how families can be torn apart by the actions of someone like my ex-husband. He was calculating and devious, and they had seen what he wanted them to see.

These thoughts came back to me some 10 years later when my sister became involved with someone similar. The difference in her case was that he was outwardly unpleasant and difficult, so everyone could see he wasn't a nice character and take action to cut him out of their lives and protect my sister.

Chapter 10

It is much more difficult for people to believe an accusation of abuse when, to them, the abuser always appears the model citizen. For me this was intensely frustrating. For years I felt so powerless, knowing that justice was just not being served.

Despite all this, even after all these years, I still love my family. I know it must have been difficult for them. I know deep down that I was loved and that they did the best they could for me at the time. Eventually they came to understand what state my ex had left the family in, and they began to reduce their contact with him. Eventually, in 2004, he walked away. He could see his support was dwindling, and after my sister, the last of us to maintain contact with him, told him she was moving to Spain, he decided to close the door to us all and leave. We never heard from him again.

I remember thinking that at last some sort of justice had prevailed, though the trail of devastation he had left behind had been unimaginable.

I do not wish to make my childhood an excuse for all of my experiences, as is so fashionable these days. Yes, it was difficult, but the important thing is that you recognise it, deal with it and move forward to build the life you want for you and your offspring. No doubt I will make my own mistakes in bringing my own children up when the time comes.

Chapter 11

A fresh start

2001 turned out to be a very good year. That autumn I met someone who would change my life, and this time very much for the better.

I was now recovering well and felt I was in a 'good place', both mentally and physically. The day I met George, I remember mentioning to a colleague that I really wasn't fussed about finding anyone new as I had all I needed in life – me and my dog Benson. And then, a few hours later, came the bolt from the blue.

George and I met at a friend's wedding reception. I knew straight away that we would eventually marry, though he took a little longer to work it out!

What struck me most about him was the way he spoke. I just knew that Spirit was with him. I remember laughing to myself because he didn't have a clue about any of that. He was a policeman, but I knew that Spirit works with each and every one of us, especially those who serve others.

The evening we met, Spirit visited me. I saw myself in a plane, taking off along a runway. The message was that things were about to take off in another way. In the vision a lady handed me a lovely ribbon-laden gift box. I immediately understood that George was being given to me. At last I felt I was getting back some of the sparkle that I had been missing from life.

I took things slowly at first, something I had never managed to do before. George had stayed single for a while, waiting for the right person to come along, so he too felt a little overwhelmed by it all.

I knew I must not bombard him with my past. He would need to know certain things about me if we were to progress as a couple, but for the most part I just wanted to enjoy our time together and put things behind me. I

Chapter 11

felt nervous talking about my previous marriage, so at first I told him only the bare minimum. He was fine about it all. I could tell that he understood most of my story, but not all of it. The truth is, no-one can ever really understand what another person has been through.

I knew I would once again need to summon all my reserves of strength to be able to make life work for the pair of us. It wasn't easy to begin with, as I found myself getting anxious on a number of occasions, but I managed to carry on. I found I was able to relax better as time went on. I'm pleased to say that I managed never to put any of my problems on to him. I know George found it difficult at times, but I think that was mainly because he had lived alone for a long time and was used to his own company.

Within a few months we had moved in together. Spirit was proud and happy for us. I would say to anyone embarking on a new relationship when you've had a rough ride with the last one that you should never expect your other half to be the knight in shining armour who will take away your problems. Only you can sort your problems out.

I now began to feel that Spirit was beginning to leave me to my own devices. It almost felt as if they were encouraging me to be more independent now George was on the scene. After all he was a policeman, so it seems appropriate to think he was sent to watch over me as Spirit had been doing. At the time it all made complete sense. I was still having some contact with Spirit, just not as much.

We got married on December 5 2005, up in the Lake District. I invited my parents. They didn't turn up, but my grandmother, aunties and cousin were there. It was a magical day, and I know Spirit was there helping us. We both deserved it.

The greatest gift of all arrived on May 18 2009, when we had our son Jacob, little 'Peeps' as we call him. I had never thought I would be able to have a child. Even for people who have led more normal lives, the arrival of a baby is a big event. For me, after everything I had been through, I just couldn't believe it.

Chapter 11

I knew the precise time of Jacob's conception. As I lay on my bed one afternoon I saw a speck of light entering my body and knew it was a child. I was astonished that I had actually seen it happen. I told George straight away, and in his usual calm manner he just said, "We'll wait and see."

Sure enough, three weeks later I learned I was pregnant. I hadn't yet had any of the usual signs of pregnancy, but as I was driving home I heard Spirit tell me that I would have a 'good pregnancy'. I bought a test kit, and when I awoke at 4 am the next morning I used it. Spirit had been right, of course - it was positive. I could hear Spirit cheering in my ear as I ran upstairs to give George the news.

We didn't sleep much after that - we were just too excited. We needed some good news then, because my beloved dog Benson had died the previous month. I had been distraught over his death. I remember thinking that although Spirit had taken something special away from me, I had been given another soul in return.

I cried my heart out when Jacob was born. Finally things were coming right for me and us as a family. I had known for the previous two years that I was to have a baby boy – I had been told by the Spirit of my grandmother. It was all part of the big plan.

However, this vision had been followed by a more serious message, which appeared to me as writings on a stone slab. It said that when my child was two years and two days old, something would happen. I knew it would be something big, but of course I had no idea what. I just put it to the back of my mind, knowing that I could do no more than wait for the day to arrive.

A new and very positive chapter was about to begin for us. On top of this we had acquired a new dog whom we named Billy, who kept us all busy in the early months. In fact he ended up being more trouble than the baby!

With most expectant mothers, the excitement of knowing a little baby

Chapter 11

is on the way overrides the fear of the impending labour. In my case, I was petrified from the minute I knew I was pregnant. I had been a midwife for a long time by now and I knew only too well what childbirth involved. All those years of encouraging home birth without pain relief went straight out of the window. Now that it was my turn, I was going to have everything!

I was also worried about how I might react if I had to undergo a traumatic delivery, as my experience of PTSD amounted to what some would describe as a mental health problem. Fortunately my consultant was very understanding. It was hard for me to explain my experience to someone I had worked with because it was so personal, but I managed to do it and it all worked out fine. My consultant never judged me or made me undergo a mental health assessment. I didn't need such a thing, as I had recovered through sheer will. But we both knew I was at increased risk of reacting badly if I had a difficult birth.

Spirit tried to allay my fears, although it wasn't until Jacob had been born that I fully understood what they been trying to tell me. They kept telling me I would be fine if I kept upright as much as possible. I panicked when I heard this, because I took it to mean I would indeed have to go through conventional labour. In fact I then learned that little Jacob was lying bum first, so I ended up having a planned caesarean section. I was elated at this news, and as my pregnancy progressed I kept willing him to stay as he was. Most people would have been getting into the all-fours position to help him turn - not me! Now I knew why Spirit had been telling me to stay up right – to keep him as he was.

Having said all that, by the time I got near my due date I had begun to feel differently. In the event I think I would have coped fine if I had to deliver him myself.

Little Jacob was born a lot smaller than expected, at 4lb 9oz, and seemed just skin and bone. The cord looked unhealthy and damaged at delivery, and clearly hadn't been letting him feed properly. His head was

Chapter 11

large in comparison to his body. Fortunately Jacob was a fighter, like his mother, and the consultant remained very relaxed about the whole issue. Thank God for that, because I didn't need any more stress.

That night, when George had gone home and I lay with Jacob in the hospital bed, I spoke to God. I had been a bit upset and kept thinking "Why me, why my little Jacob?" Straight away I heard a man's voice saying, "Worry not child, all will be well." I felt very relieved, and we fell asleep in each other's arms.

Jacob soon started to thrive, but I began to discover that he was no ordinary child. Almost immediately after I got him home, I started noticing that he would look at invisible things over my shoulder or behind my head and laugh. George had begun to notice it too. Whoever or whatever he could see seemed to make him giggle, even within a couple of days of being born. I had looked after thousands of children, yet I had never seen this before.

Then I began to see another very strange thing - specks of light around him, especially at night. I knew Jacob was special. He could clearly see Spirit. Perhaps I should not have been so surprised, because I was now following a very spiritual pathway myself. I loved the fact that we could both see Spirit and felt the two of us were just meant to be together, and I was the ideal person to encourage him to flourish and develop.

In the early days poor George never really got a look in, but he was really good at all the practical things that needed doing, whereas I was the one who encouraged Jacob to be emotionally and spiritually the person he was.

In the event the message I had seen on the stone slab turned out to be spot on. On May 20 2011, we were told that little Jacob had been diagnosed with cerebral palsy. Life is never going to be easy for us, but if anything it has made me love him even more.

I consider myself fortunate that my experiences in life, the knowledge I have accumulated through my trials and the qualifications I have gained have enabled me to go forward with the confidence I need to care for

Chapter 11

Jacob. Above everything I wanted to be the best parent possible for him. Perhaps I have realised more than most the importance of raising a child so that he will leave me, when the time comes, to venture forth with the confidence and life skills he will need to survive in the world.

This self-discovery taught me a lot about myself and how I needed to make changes for the better. So often people have children because it's what society expects, or to fill the void of a past in which love has been lacking. But we should have children for the right reasons. They are born pure. It is our parenting that sets the blueprint for their lives and determines their chances of becoming loving and productive beings.

If you had a rough childhood, it does not mean your opportunities will be less – in fact such people are often extremely independent and have a resilience that will take them far. A harsh upbringing can motivate you, push you on to achieve what you want in life. However, it doesn't always work this way. Many children I have worked with have clearly been hindered in their lives by their upbringing, and it is these children my heart goes out to the most.

Parenting is the most important job you will ever do. Children don't come with an instruction manual. Nobody can tell you how difficult a challenge it can be, especially when you suffers years of sleep deprivation.

Being a good parent is far from easy, but it helps if you have learned to give and accept love yourself. Over the years I have studied a lot of research into the effects of the different parenting styles people adopt. It interests me because of what happened to me. Like many others, I feel I didn't benefit from the level of emotional investment a child needs, and that I suffered the consequences of that in later life.

Unfortunately, unless you can gain an understanding of what children need from a source outside your own family, all you have to go on is what happened to you when you were little. You end up replaying your own upbringing, and the cycle begins again. Spirit have told me that they see the devastating consequences of abusive upbringing and have encouraged me to include this discussion in my book.

Too often when a child goes off the rails, parents will take no responsibility for the problem, or deny it has anything to do with them. As a health professional I constantly see families blighted by childhood behavioural problems which can be put down to parenting failures. I have seen three-year-olds who are unable to walk because their days are spent belted into a buggy while their parents go about their lives oblivious to their growing child's developmental needs.

Research shows that parents adopt different styles according to how they were brought up themselves. The authoritarian approach is usually adopted by people who were themselves brought up in a very strict household. Such children live in a world where they are expected to be seen and not heard, to follow strict rules without questioning them. The parents are highly demanding and controlling and display low levels of responsiveness to the child's needs. Children brought up like this fail to develop the interpersonal skills which are so vital to achieve happiness and success in life.

We know that early social interactions in the family provide the foundation for the development of social skills that will eventually be used to interact with others outside the family. If this foundation is weak or absent, children will be at a disadvantage compared to their peers. I can relate to this - I had very poor social skills when I was young and I know it was because I lacked the confidence to interact properly with others. People suffering from anxiety-related illnesses will usually also come into this category.

The opposite style is the permissive approach, where parents allow their children to grow up in an environment of extreme freedom and flexibility. This can also be damaging, because a childhood without boundaries can leave a child unprepared for environments where boundaries do exist, such as school and work. They may not understand or respond well to mainstream behaviour and will struggle when it comes to socialising with others. They often exhibit low self-esteem. Children who are allowed to do what they want may also develop feelings of insecurity, because of a perception that their parents don't care what happens to them. The best balance is provided by the 'assertive-democratic style', which can be characterised by high degrees of responsiveness by the parent to the child. Such parents set firm limits on what their children are allowed to do, while listening to their needs. They will negotiate and reason with their children to enable them to understand why certain behaviour is expected. They expect their children to be independent and to be able to think for themselves, but define acceptable and unacceptable behaviour.

These parents communicate properly with their children, which enables them in turn to develop good communication and social skills. Research has shown that children whose parents adopt this style tend to have the best cognitive and social skills and are the most emotionally well-adjusted.

The key to all this lies in parents understanding the importance of being responsive to their children. Research tells us that sensitive, responsive care in the early years is extremely important to the quality of a person's later life. When a parent tunes in to an infant's communication signals, interprets them correctly and responds in ways that meet the child's needs, the child is much more likely to respond, display signs of secure attachment (a close and loving relationship) and exhibit better behavioural and emotional adjustments in later life.

This healthy relationship between parent and child is crucial in developing specific brain pathways to follow the 'correct' behaviour, as infants are unable to do this on their own. The process starts even before birth. Children suffering stress in the womb because of physical conditions or because the mother is experiencing extreme stress, such as domestic abuse, will often be born with very high levels of cortisol, the fight-or-flight hormone which the body produces in response to stress. These babies may be twitchy and over-anxious as infants.

Chapter 11

I have cared for many a child like this. I experienced the problem first-hand with my own son, which taught me a great deal about how infants can be affected by such circumstances. When Jacob was born it was obvious that he had been starved in the womb for some time. I believe he stopped growing at 32 weeks, although he was not born until 39 weeks. He appeared stressed and anxious, as if he had got used to in an environment that wasn't giving him what he needed. I knew from the start that he would need extra special care.

I soon began to notice his increased sensitivity to almost anything. We couldn't make journeys with him in the car seat, as he couldn't tolerate the noise, lights and activity round him. It was almost as if he wanted to be cocooned, with as little stimulation as possible, while he recuperated and gained strength. Trying to join parent groups was a nightmare, because he could only tolerate about 10 minutes of all the goings on before we had to leave.

I did manage to learn baby massage at classes run by a good friend of mine, and slowly but surely this helped him to relax and begin enjoying life. You could see the change taking place before your eyes. George and I worked round the clock to be responsive loving parents. I dread to think how he would have turned out in the wrong hands.

One time when he wasn't feeding very well, my late grandmother told me in a dream to send him lots of love while giving him his feeds. We did this, and almost immediately he started to feed better and pack the weight on. Despite an initial rather poor prognosis for his development, he is now catching up slowly but surely and making progress. He has been diagnosed with nystagmus and is partially sighted but I think he sees better than they say, especially when he wants something and your some distance away – his focus is a little vague but he appears to make out who you are to grab your attention. He has come so far because he has been loved through it all. You can never spoil a child with too much love, and Spirit says children will always flourish with love. Love conquers all. At two

Chapter 11

years old, Jacob is a happy child who laughs and loves in abundance, and for that we are truly grateful.

Chapter 12

The journey home

These days, 12 years on, I find it hard to believe I went through such an ordeal. In fact I consider myself living testament to the fact that we are all capable of surviving the most horrendous experiences. I would never have imagined, back in the days when I could barely bring myself to go outside, that I would marry again, have a family and live a normal, fulfilled life.

The completeness of my recovery has been underlined by two promotions at work, which eventually led to my becoming a specialist public health nurse. In 2009 I gained a Bachelor of Science degree. I was even nominated for the prize of best academic achievement in a field of 80 graduates. Not bad for a person whose brain, not so long ago, was periodically shutting down to enable itself to heal!

It's been an incredible journey. I think I could now give the medics a run for their money on the subject of natural self-healing.

Could I have got better faster with medical help? I will never know. My gut instinct tells me that it probably wouldn't have helped much, because relying on medication would have distracted me from what I really needed to do - to look inside myself and draw on my own inner resources of strength, character and determination.

My life now is completely different to the one I once led. It is quieter, gentler and much more peaceful. Of course I still have to manage stressful events, as we all do, but I find these days that I can handle most of them as easily as making a cup of tea. Far from living like a hermit to avoid the risk of any kind of stress, I find I have developed an increased tolerance to stressful situations. Having been through what I did, the everyday causes of stress which most people get frazzled about simply don't touch me.

I feel proud of having been able to defy medical theory and challenge

Chapter 12

the stigma attached to those who have suffered from a supposed mental illness. I have learned that we all have it in us to be survivors. All you need to do is believe in yourself and have a desire to get better.

My experiences have helped me to develop an exceptional level of independence. For example, I drove myself home five days after giving birth to Jacob by c-section. Not that I would recommend this to anyone else, but I give it as an example of my increased tolerance to pain and stress. I never felt any pain because I was able to keep it under control mentally.

I'm not invincible, of course. I do get tired easily. More than most people, I find I need to give myself periods of rest to keep my batteries charged and my body healthy. If I don't, my energy levels drop too far and I start to feel low. I have found this difficult to cope with, as I used to be able to take tiredness in my stride.

For this reason I began to find work difficult at times, and in the end I had to accept that full-time work was not for me. I also wanted to jump off the bandwagon of a professional career and enjoy my life and health more, because I had been taking it very much for granted. For me, a healthy balance allows me to continue to work, earn enough money and keep my independence. This has been enormously important to me, as it is through my work that I feel I can help others who are faced with difficulties. My experience has enabled me to relate particularly well to others' problems and given me an increased level of understanding of the people I care for.

The pledge I make to myself now is that I will not tolerate bad or unfair behaviour of the kind I once had to endure. Domestic violence is not going to go away. The statistics suggest that one woman in four suffers from it at some point, while there is a growing problem for men too. One in six men now say they experience domestic abuse.

No doubt some men have always tended to abuse their partners, but I doubt whether we would find much in the historical record about men being on the receiving end of such behaviour. It's hard to believe now, but

Chapter 12

up until the 20th century it was perfectly legal for a husband to beat his wife with a stick for failing in her duties towards him, domestic or personal. Women who had to bear the hardship of childbirth and bringing up the family could be abused and injured perfectly legally, just for allowing the wrong man into their lives.

Perhaps the rising rates of violence by women towards men suggest an escalating epidemic of what I would call societal abuse. Many shops and public buildings display notices warning against the use of abusive behaviour towards staff, something you would never see in decades gone by. I think we can safely say that we are a long way from being a civil and kind society. There are still so many prejudices, discriminations and false judgments flying around that it is sometimes hard to believe we are living in the 21st century.

Having worked in the NHS for 20 years now, I more than most can appreciate, through the stories they have told me, the difficulties people have to cope with in their everyday lives. It saddens me that people who face the most extraordinary adversity in their lives are stigmatised and subjected to terrible judgements. It applies to the homeless, the disabled, the visually impaired and people living with chronic illnesses, to mention but a few, and often with the added burden of poverty. These people need great strength to survive.

I cannot count the number of times I have seen people display superior attitudes and pass judgement on those less fortunate than themselves. I want to say to them - who are you to judge others, and make their lives even more difficult?

We could learn so much from the way such people deal with their challenges, because in truth they are really very special individuals. I talk to many people who have faced the most extraordinary adversity, and they always say that they wouldn't want it any other way, because their experiences have made them the person they are. Adversity, I believe, can be the making of you.

Chapter 12

If you are one of those who look down on others in worse circumstances than yourself, I would urge you to take stock now, because you will be coming back in another lifetime to learn how to fix and overcome your prejudices. This is the way things are dealt with spiritually. It's true what they say – "What goes around comes around".

The last 12 years has been an incredible journey. Although I wasn't exactly thankful at the time for all the difficulties I had to face, at least I can look back now in good health and feel it was worth it. I learned such a lot about the way our bodies can and do recover. I felt my body healing and repairing itself. I knew when to stop everything and take a break, because my body told me to. The brain is an amazing organ – I know from the way mine healed itself. I had to put the work in, of course. I had to retrain my brain to think and act differently. I had to develop the life skills I needed to stay healthy. I developed assertiveness skills which enabled me to feel more in control of my life, instead of living with continuing insecurities and anxiety.

I know many people will question the spiritual experiences I had. Yet they have been only too real, and they continue to this day. If anything they have become even more vivid.

I continue to have some direct contact with the spirit world on a weekly basis. It's almost as if they like you to know they are still around and will visit in times of need.

Only a few months ago they came back to give me some reassurance regarding my son's health. It was at a time when I was very concerned about his mental and physical development. He had been born small and frail and was not reaching his milestones. Although I had tried to remain positive for his sake, I still kept experiencing the fear of not knowing.

Then one night, Spirit showed me my little boy suddenly standing tall and walking towards me. At the time it was so real that I let out a shriek of excitement. He had never crawled or rolled at that point and was only just managing to sit up unsupported at the time, but right on cue, some

Chapter 12

four days after the dream, he stood up and, with a little support, took some steps.

Then, at a time when I was very down about family circumstances and my son's health, my beloved Benson came back to visit me. We had been in and out of hospital with Jacob after he had had a horrendous bout of pneumonia. I remember drifting off to sleep and then suddenly being dropped into a little room. The door swung open and there before me stood Benson. He bounded up to me and nearly knocked me over with the joy and excitement. It was just like the old days. His face and features and his long and flowing coat were so real. It was so lovely to relieve the memory of his appearance and personality, something which so easily fades over the years.

Of all the experiences I have had over the years, that is probably the most memorable. I consider myself very lucky to have been given that. I woke up feeling much lighter of heart.

I don't consider myself to be anybody special. I don't look at myself as anything other than a trained nurse and midwife. I know there are many others out there who do far more than me.

I do believe that every one of us is born with the gift of hearing, seeing, and feeling the Spirit or God force which surrounds us. It's just that most of us lose the gift, and only tend to experience things of a spiritual nature when tragedy strikes. I always think that's a great pity.

The millennium has brought about change for us all, with our consciousnesses heightened to a newer and deeper spiritual level. This is borne out by the growing interest in meditative practice over the past 10 years. Apart from opening yourself up for more spiritual experiences through meditation, the health benefits are enormous.

More and more people are trying to achieve a better work/life balance and looking to live a quieter and more peaceful life. We are all being encouraged to look back at the days when life used to be so much simpler and happier, without all the trappings and pressures of modern existence. There is an increasing interest in using the land to grow our own food and

Chapter 12

produce, as our forefathers did. These are all examples of how our consciousnesses are being developed towards a more straightforward and spiritual way of life, offering us the tranquillity to withdraw from the busy modern world through meditation or prayer.

I believe many more people will experience the presence of Spirit in their lives in the years to come, and I hope this book will help others to do so. You may, like me, begin to experience the gentle signs of contact by the spirit world, such as the subtle force or visual aura I experienced during sleep. Don't be afraid, as Spirit will only allow this to happen to you gradually, and you will be given time to become comfortable with their presence. Stay strong, and if you feel the need for guidance and support, the spiritualist churches are always ready to offer it. Even better, enrol in one of the development classes that are held up and down the country. It will help you to understand some of your experiences.

Turning to the spiritual side of life is not always an easy road to take. With any sort of knowledge comes responsibility. You will begin to see that there is more to the world than you thought. You will realise that each of us has a responsibility to act in a way that encourages humanity, justice and above all love towards our fellow men.

Once you're on the spiritual pathway, you will be encouraged to look within yourself for ways of improving your life and those of others. Where once you might have turned a blind eye to the injustices shown to others, you will be encouraged to speak out and fight for what is right and good in the world. All this comes at a price – you may expect others to fight you bitterly, as less enlightened people will always be shown up and made to feel inadequate with such goodness around them. Show them, move on and above all learn to protect yourself. A simple prayer each morning will help you to keep safe from harm.

Leading a more spiritual way of life isn't just about pursuing peace yourself, although it will help you to remain grounded. It's more about

Chapter 12

how you can serve others and the world around you. The troubles of the world have become very serious, and it is our responsibility to try to reshape the world into one we can hand on to the generations to come. We all have a responsibility to set a blueprint for the behaviours and attitudes of our children.

You may find as you set about adopting a more spiritual way of life that people will tend to either love you or loathe you for it. While you may inspire some, others will not like the way you behave. Wherever I have been, in both work and social situations, there have always been a few people who have tried to put me down, to make me unhappy. I have never let them succeed. I believe you will always experience this jealousy, no matter what you do. So alert have I become to this that I need only be in the company of someone like this for a few seconds to detect their negative vibrations. I will then withdraw.

The simpler life I have learned to live now may make people feel you are a little naïve. I think it's the opposite - the more humbly and quietly you lead your life, the wiser you are. They say a wise man speaks very little. I now feel a lot more comfortable with myself, thanks to gaining a deeper inner understanding of how and why things happen, including bad things.

I know it is difficult for many people who suffer great pain to believe in a god. I went through a long period of hating God and Spirit because of what happened to me, and in despair at the evil deeds people do to each other. But in truth it isn't God who does these things - we do them ourselves. He doesn't instruct people to be malevolent and cause suffering to others – we do that to each other, each and every day. Yet we always seem to put the blame elsewhere, instead of accepting and changing ourselves.

Spirit tells me that we all know our life plan before we come to this earth - we just forget about it when we arrive. I believe however that some

Chapter 12

of us do remember our life plan to some extent, and may even prepare for their own passing when they are fit and young and there appears to be no reason why they should die for many years. One example of this was the 9/11 tragedy. A recently-published book called Messages, signs, visits and premonitions from loved ones lost on 9/11, by Bonnie McEneaney, was dedicated to some of the people who apparently knew they were going to die that awful day. The stories are remarkable. Many of them had made preparations beforehand because they somehow knew that their time here on earth was coming to an end. They must have known that they were only meant to be here for a short time. It isn't always like this of course - it's usually more difficult for people to understand why tragedies happen, especially when children are involved.

I don't believe such people suffer the way we imagine they might do before they die. I truly believe that they are relieved of a lot of their suffering through a mental and physical shutting down process by Spirit. Even when I was experiencing the most horrendous mental abuse, I felt as if it was happening to someone else. It was almost as if protective barriers were put around me. I believe our own bodies protect us from harm as well.

It is sad that some poor children have to suffer at the hands of others so that we stupid adults will learn from it. If we were more spiritually advanced and lived in a kinder, more caring world, it just wouldn't happen.

We are now experiencing a great spiritual renaissance, and we have been afforded an opportunity to grow and learn as individuals. It is a very challenging time for us and the world as a whole. The millennium has brought us a deeper understanding of the world and the situations we find ourselves in. It's almost as if we have shed a layer of our arrogance and come closer to understanding other people. I believe we are at last beginning to develop a greater appreciation of the world around us. The rates of depression and mental illness have increased fourfold in recent

Chapter 12

years, because people are experiencing greater extremes within their lives. The truth is, we need to have these feelings if we are to make things better for us all and generations to come.

We are a long way from where we need to be, but I do believe we are making great advances towards this goal of connection and enlightenment. In the process we will all be collectively cared for by the God force and the love that surrounds us, a love which is now gathering momentum. Ultimately I believe we will be rewarded with the joy that is there for us all to experience and that Spirit will balance the scales for us.

I got through my own experience by sheer will and determination, receiving that little bit of extra help and support that was needed to get me back on track. For that I feel blessed and thankful.

Spirit says that no prayer or cry for help ever goes unheard. You get back the help that is suited to your spiritual needs and individual make-up. For some it may just be a friend ringing at the right time to give you a hug or a word of comfort, but you will always be helped and supported in some way.

Even if we think no-one walks beside us as we tread our path through life, we must always remember and take comfort from the fact that we are never, ever, really alone.

The end

www.ingramcontent.com/pod-product-compliance
Lightning Source LLC
Chambersburg PA
CBHW071517040426
42444CB00008B/1682